Workplace Neuro

Rethinking workplace policy & culture to include people with diverse brains and create workplaces where both NeuroDivergent (and NeuroTypical) Team Members can shine

Written by Lyric Lark Rivera,

NeuroDivergent Rebel

Illustrations by David Rivera

Workplace NeuroDiversity Rising

Lyric Rivera

Published by Lyric Rivera, 2022.

WORKPLACE NEURODIVERSITY RISING

First edition. November 23, 2022.

Copyright © 2022 Lyric Rivera.

ISBN: 979-8215235652

Written by Lyric Rivera.

I dedicate this book to my love and partner, David, who was by my side before my diagnosis when corporate life almost killed me, despite my disengagement for many years due to the extreme burnout and mental health crisis I faced. In addition, I would like to dedicate this book to my friends, loved ones, mentors, readers, viewers, Patreons Subscribers, Facebook Supporters, YouTube Channel Members, Twitter Super Followers, and anyone else who's ever supported and believed in me along the way. Without you, this book would not be possible. Finally, I would like to dedicate this book to all of the previous employers I've ever had, both good and bad. Thanks to the bad for giving me enough examples of what businesses can do wrong to fill a book, and to the good for restoring my faith that there are kind people out there.

Intro: What IS NeuroDiversity?

NeuroDiversity = ALL Brains NeuroDivergent & NeuroTypical working together & supporting each other.

Neurodiversity is a term coined and conceptualized in the late 1990s by Judy Singer, an Autistic sociologist. Judy argued that diverse neurological conditions and learning disabilities (such as Autism, dyslexia, dyscalculia, hyperlexia, dyspraxia, ADHD, obsessive-compulsive disorder (OCD), and Tourette syndrome (TS)—ALL of which are more common in NeuroDivergent people) are the result of normal variations in human brain type. I like to say they're all just different shades of humanity.

NeuroDiversity is all about celebrating, empowering, and accepting the natural differences between human brains; whether it's the differences we're born with (like Autism, ADHD, & dyslexia) or differences we develop in life (such as PTSD, cPTSD, anxiety, and other mental health conditions). Regardless of how these brain differences originate, the brain's owners all experience the world differently from those who are considered "NeuroTypical".

Society's systems (school systems, healthcare systems, public spaces, and workplace systems), have all been set up by NeuroTypical people—what you might call the NeuroMajority. This has been harmful (albeit it usually unintentionally) to people like me

Who am I? More on that in a moment.

Unfortunately, NeuroDivergent people weren't given the opportunity to give input to NeuroTypical people when they were developing these systems. For a long time, NeuroDivergent people have been told the systems were fine, and we were broken.

People around us are always asking us to try harder to fit ourselves into systems and spaces that weren't designed with our needs in mind, instead of improving them to create more flexibility and inclusivity. This is both cruel and unfair.

Many people in the workforce today are NeuroDivergent and often don't even know it.

I didn't find out I was Autistic until I was 29 years old, and my ADHD wasn't officially diagnosed until several years later, in my mid 30's. So I spent a LARGE part of my life not knowing or understanding how and why my mind worked so differently from those of the people around me.

Who am I, and why do I care so much about NeuroDiversity?

My name is Lyric Rivera and I'm multiply NeuroDivergent, but I didn't know this fact for most of my life. I'm also nonbinary and use gender neutral pronouns (they/them).

For almost thirty years, I thought I was just an inferior NeuroTypical person. When, a few months before my thirtieth birthday, I found out I was Autistic, I started studying NeuroDiversity.

This changed my life.

Up until that point I'd managed to scrape by, forcing myself to functioning as society expected me to, until situations changed, or my ability to do so ran out, and I was no longer able to keep up with the demands the world had for me.

In order to show up and be the best version of myself, I needed the freedom to flex the NeuroTypical systems and expectations, and do things differently.

Learning more about NeuroDiversity has allowed me to stop holding myself to NeuroTypical standards, and given me the confidence to better advocate for my needs, setting me free to be authentically, radically, boldly, and proudly, myself.

I'm just one of many who have had to make their way in a world where traditional methods of education and employment didn't suit us. I've had to learn how to create my own channels, when the way forward was blocked by a NeuroTypical system.

In high school, rather than planning for university, I took my first full time job, as soon as I was legally able, after years of working in the family business under my mother's watchful eye. Taking the long way around has helped me to develop a diverse business background, and my experiences have helped inform my knowledge of NeuroTypical systems, and how to create new channels.

Lessons learned in life

I didn't know about the differences in my brain when I entered the workforce in my preteens, helping my mom with the family business—a hair salon; but working there enabled me to gain many of the skills I would need to succeed in other workplaces.

Starting at around age 11, I learned how to take care of a wide variety of tasks around the hair salon I grew up in, from sweeping floors and taking out the trash, to shampooing clients and booking appointments. Eventually, I was even preparing the bank deposits at the end of each day.

Bit by bit, I mastered inventory control, customer service, and even the basics behind running a business and bookkeeping.

By the time I was ready to apply for my first job outside of the family business, at the age of 16, I had already accumulated a nice set of workplace skills and was ahead of the game when compared to most high school (and many college) students.

My next job—my first venture out into the working world without a family cushion—

would be in fast food, as a roller-skating car-hop for a popular American fast food restaurant chain.

Over the course of five years, I worked my way up to an assistant manager's position, soaking up as much free leadership training as possible along the way, before moving on at the age of twenty-one.

Following this, about a year before the crash of 2008, I was working in the Materials Management Library of one of the world's largest computer manufacturers. I was one of the first people to ever hold a one terabyte hard drive—when most of the world could barely imagine such a thing existed.

This environment was sensory-friendly: perfect for an undiagnosed Autistic Person who was completely unaware of their sensory needs.

What is sensory-friendly? The specifics vary from person to person but, in broad strokes, it's an environment in which the sensory needs of a person are met. This could be anything from a lack of noise and light, to being able to communicate via computer rather than on the phone.

For me, what I found myself in was a mostly silent room, naturally lit, with the lights above my desk not too bright. We were all allowed to listen to music on headphones during the day while we worked, and things were orderly because everyone meticulously followed the rules.

At the end of the day, I would arrive home feeling calm and relaxed, instead of harried, stressed, and exhausted. It was almost perfect, until it ended very suddenly in 2008 when the economy crashed and almost 9000 people in the company lost their jobs.

After my time at the computer company, I moved through a few other jobs that weren't nearly as meaningful—or accommodating to my needs.

By the time I was twenty-five, in addition to working in fast food, I'd had jobs waiting tables, working for the state of Texas as a contractor, and as a retail store manager specializing in marketing and visual merchandising.

I landed what I thought was my dream job in my mid-twenties, working in a hip and trendy office. At the time, my brain differences were still unknown to me, and I wouldn't find out the truth until several years later.

Unfortunately, some employers expect the employee to overcome any and all weaknesses they have, or be working towards eliminating them (mostly or entirely without any help from the company), which may not be possible or healthy for someone with a disability or learning difference.

In addition, NeuroTypical people (those considered to have "average" brains) are often used as an unfair benchmark for NeuroDivergent people. It's like comparing fish to cats, then getting mad at the cat for not being able to breath under water, or being upset with the fish for not being able to climb a tree.

NeuroDivergent people literally have different brains, we are built to work differently, and asking us to mimic and hold ourselves to NeuroTypical standards does a huge disservice to us.

Strengths and weaknesses are not inherently either good nor bad, they're simply part of the human experience. But, where NeuroTypical people are in a system geared towards boosting their strengths and working with their weaknesses, NeuroDivergent people all too often find themselves in the opposite position.

Mistakes are also not something to fear: they are opportunities for learning and growth—but many organizations have cultures that don't leave room for life's happy accidents. This is a culture which unfairly affects the NeuroDivergent.

When members of an organization become risk averse and afraid to be vulnerable and honest with their weaknesses, they are less likely to try new things or ask for help when they need it, because of how taboo it can become to make mistakes or ask for help in these environments—thus stifling creativity: a box which NeuroDivergent people often find impossible to work within.

From a NeuroDivergent perspective, it is hard when you struggle to do things that others find easy, especially if you don't know why you are struggling.

I wanted so badly to get things right, but people around me were always telling me that I needed to try harder when I had already been doing my very best. So I learned to push and push, until I failed or burned out.

This type of pushing eventually led me to my first significant burnout of adulthood and, ultimately, my realisation that I was Autistic.

Life A.A.D. (After Autism Discovery)

It's hard to leave a secure job.

The job that burnt me out wasn't difficult. Technically, it should have been easy (not to mention below my skill level), if I had been properly accommodated.

It was a stable job, and had great perks (401k, insurance, unlimited PTO, etc.), but they couldn't accommodate me and that made what should have been easy, very taxing.

All the extras in the world are irrelevant if they come at the cost of your mental and physical health.

So I left the "good corporate job", in search of an employer who would empower me.

My next job would be with a company that specialized in HR and business consulting.

Although legally, you should not have to mention details of your disability during the early stages of the interview, I disclosed that I was Autistic early in the interview process and was upfront with the accommodations I would need to be an all-star employee.

When I let the consulting firm know that I would need to work remotely, instead of saying "That's not how we do things" because they had no remote employees before my ask, my new employer met my request with curiosity, asking how I planned to effectively work from the comfort of my own home.

Because I had a carefully thought-out plan for how I could work more effectively from home than in any office, and I promised that allowing me to do so would produce amazing work quality, I was permitted to become the organization's first remote employee.

In 2019 I began to design and deliver corporate trainings on Autistic Inclusion and Workplace Neurodiversity on behalf of the consulting firm. It was my favorite task so far, but was still not my primary focus, as I held the title VP of Marketing and had many additional responsibilities.

In the early spring of 2020 I was gearing up to fly around the country and speak about my experiences as an openly NeuroDivergent business professional, as part of a launch for a new NeuroDiversity initiative for the consulting firm. However, in March of 2020, when the COVID pandemic reached the United States, everything changed very quickly.

One by one, the flights and conferences were canceled or moved to Zoom.

Organizations all over the world began to trim budgets and lay people off. COVID-19 hit Learning and Development teams hard, and I was let go when we had to adjust our service lines to compensate for the rapid changes in the volatile economy.

We cried together on the termination call that was done over Zoom.

I have no hard feelings towards the firm. In fact, I still worked with my former employer on a few projects as an independent contractor, in the months after being let go.

I still communicate with my old boss from time to time. I have great love for her, and always will.

Forced to Fly

For the first time in my life, being let go didn't send me into a panic. I expected to feel fear, but instead, I felt free. It felt "right."

In hindsight, I'm truly grateful that I was let go, because, due to my NeuroDivergent tendency to struggle with change, and my fierce loyalty to the members of my team, I would likely not have made this move on my own.

The spiraling global economy turned out to be just the nudge I needed to force me to try something risky: working on my own.

From fast food and retail, to tech, corporate, and hospitality, I've weaved my way in and out of multiple industries and titles.

Over the years I've worked in management, executive leadership, customer service, and project management, and I've thoroughly enjoyed working in operations, recruiting, HR, and employee relations. But out of all of the types of work that I've done over the years, my absolute favorite task at any job has always been teaching others.

I've found a new freedom and ease in working for myself, managing my schedule, and accommodating my needs as I see fit.

Other people, and the pressures they bring, stress me out. Working on my own, and having full control helps me to be firm in asserting my boundaries.

I'm not opposed to re-entering the workforce as an employee and having the stability that comes with being employed by someone else, but most employers at this point in time simply aren't willing to give me the amount of freedom and control that I need to be the best version of myself.

The Heart of the Problem

There are specific changes that need to be made to most workplaces to make them truly accessible for minds like mine. Unfortunately, many business owners are stuck in their old ways of doing things.

NeuroDivergent people are already in the workforce, though it is likely that many of us are still under or unemployed. NeuroDiversity is the next frontier in Diversity and Inclusion. If your D&I program doesn't take all NeuroDivergent people into account, it's already obsolete.

Don't worry. It's not too late to get things on track. Every day the clock resets, and we have the chance to start over and get ourselves moving in the right direction.

About this Guide

Having a supportive environment can be the difference between employee success and failure, and when we support the diverse minds within an organization, everyone on the team benefits (because much of what is necessary for NeuroDivergent success will benefit everyone in a company, and diversity brings other perspectives, skills, and ideas that a workplace geared solely towards NeuroTypical people simply can't).

That's why I've written this handy guide for you. The purpose of this book is to help empower other people and organizations to consider what they can do to support NeuroDivergent employees, and provide practical ways to begin.

My goal is to outline things, and make this process so easy that there are no excuses not to start making these changes right away.

I want to arm you with information, so that you may become a champion of NeuroDiversity within your organization, or an ally who can effectively amplify NeuroDivergent voices.

This book is designed to be read front to back, but is also arranged in sections, to allow you to skip to your company's specific problem areas (since every organization is unique). I've also included a handy glossary of terms at the back of this book, for easy reference.

I DO recommend that you start out by reading through the section titled "" before you start jumping or skipping between the other sections of this guide. After that, go wherever you feel you need to.

"What are my organization's problem areas? How can I figure that out?"

Keep reading the "" section below, or skip to the "" section, to learn more. Both of these will help you start to figure out the right answers.

Getting Started

An inclusive organizational culture is one where every team member can come to work feeling supported, appreciated, encouraged, and empowered by their environment. Feeling safe and seen, your employees—both NeuroDivergent and NeuroTypical—will be able to bring their best game.

Unfortunately, some of the problems preventing inclusivity can be as invisible as our differences (unless we do a little digging).

This book is intended to help you better understand how all employees (NeuroDivergent & NeuroTypical) experience organizational culture. It will also provide information about addressing some of the most common problems areas that prevent the genuine inclusion of people whose minds work differently.

Remember, NeuroDiversity includes ALL brains, NeuroDivergent and NeuroTypical. These processing and cognitive differences should not be an afterthought when building or making changes to an organization.

Prerequisites

There are many ways people within a workplace can be diverse. Most often when we hear about diversity in the workplace, conversations are around racial and gender-based issues. However, there are many additional forms of diversity, both visible and invisible, that can and should be considered when creating diverse teams (gender, orientation, age, disability status, or NeuroDivergence—to name just a few).

Creating true inclusion means creating an environment where everyone feels safe and supported, and is able to show up as their best and most authentic self, because of the support and understanding they receive (or can reasonably expect to receive) from the people around them.

This guide is intended to help you look at one, often overlooked, piece of the diversity and inclusion "pie": NeuroDiversity. However, there are many areas not covered in this manual that must be considered in your organization, in order to be truly inclusive.

NeuroDiversity is a form of (mostly) invisible diversity that occurs in all intersections of the population. People of any age, race, gender, or orientation can be NeuroDivergent, meaning those with intersecting identities are likely to face more challenges than those who are not multiply marginalized.

Additionally, NeuroDivergent people are more likely to consider themselves LGBTQIA+ than NeuroTypical people are, for a variety of reasons. Therefore, this is a major area of intersectionality that should be evaluated alongside your NeuroDiversity initiative.

"Autistic adults and adolescents are approximately eight times more likely to identify as asexual and 'other' sexuality than their non-autistic peers"[1] and "People who do not identify with the sex they were assigned at birth are three to six times as likely to be autistic as cisgender people are"[2].

---

1. https://www.cam.ac.uk/research/news/autistic-individuals-are-more-likely-to-be-lgbtq

2. https://www.spectrumnews.org/news/largest-study-to-date-confirms-overlap-between-autism-and-gender-diversity/

Below are some examples of additional forms of diversity that organizations need to be mindful of when working towards their goals of being truly inclusive:

- Age.

- Race / ethnicity / national origin.

- LGBTQIA+ inclusion.

- Disability status - physical disabilities / cognitive, mental health, or other invisible disabilities.

- Citizenship status.

- Personal / religious beliefs.

- Education / income (e.g. grew up with wealth or from a low-income household).

- Criminal background.

If your organization has not already considered the areas above, you may have additional work to do before the items in the following chapters can be effectively implemented.

Step 1: Finding Out Where You Stand & Facing Problem Areas Head On

Using an Organizational Survey to Gain Input from Your Team.

Although there are some common pain points in almost any company, every organization is as unique as the living, breathing, humans working within them.

For many years, organizations have been viewed by many as machines, with processes and systems that pump out work or products.

However, as a human who has worked within many of these varied organizational systems, I have noticed a BIG problem with this type of thinking in regards to organizational culture.

When organizational leaders view their businesses as machines, and their employees as parts in them (instead of viewing them as people), they forget the human aspect of business. Treating people like machines does them a huge disservice by both dehumanizing them, and contributing to exploitative work cultures.

Organizations are made out of living breathing people, who have real needs, feelings and emotions...machines are not.

When we view our organization as a machine, it means not treating people like humans; treating them instead like disposable resources, or parts of the machine, burning them out and discarding them when they grow tired of the abuse.

However, workplace burnout will often impact your most loyal, top performers.

People viewing their organization like a machine fail to realize that the machine parts who burn out in the workplace, both NeuroDivergent or NeuroTypical, tend to be some of the most devoted employees. Why? Because to work hard enough to burn out, you have to care about what you're doing.

People who don't care don't push themselves or bother expending extra energy, they do the bare minimum.

A dedicated NeuroDivergent employee's risk of burnout rises exponentially, especially if the environment isn't accommodating, and they cannot get their needs met.

These needs are more than just workplace accommodations. The needs of any individual human being are more complex than that. For example:

❖ Emotional safety, through true inclusion.

❖ Being heard and understood.

❖ Enough freedom to do things in a way that works best for the individual.

❖ Autonomy, career advancement, and respect.

Too many NeuroDiversity and Disability Hiring initiatives create separate pipelines for NeuroDivergent people and those with disabilities, requiring the person going through the program to out themselves in order to access the resources available to them. This both assumes a person knows that they have a disability (remember I didn't find out I was Autistic until I was 29, and my ADHD wasn't discovered until I was in my mid 30's), and segregates them before they even get a chance to show their abilities.

In addition, these programs are so often focused on entry level jobs, temp jobs, and other low paying work, with little to no advancement opportunities for the candidates within them (another reason people may not feel safe outing themselves: worrying they may be limiting their career growth opportunities by exposing themselves and their differences).

What do you, an organizational leader, manager, HR professional, or NeuroDivergent employee, do first, and where should you start?

First, you have to find out where you stand, by looking more deeply at the organizational culture, policies, procedures, and by getting open and honest feedback from the members of your organization.

There are multiple ways you can solicit feedback, however anonymous organizational surveys would be my strong recommendation, because they allow for people to give candid feedback without fear of repercussions.

Depending on your organization's unique culture, people may or may not feel comfortable airing their grievances openly in meetings or public forums. Ironically, you may not know if people feel unsafe if you don't ask them anonymously.

Organizational surveys are designed to help shine a light on the hidden problems likely to prevent current and future NeuroDivergent team members from feeling supported and able to thrive within your organization.

Results from a well-designed organizational survey should help you to understand better how NeuroDivergent employees experience your organizational culture. Each team member's input should give you better direction and a better understanding of the current organizational dynamics.

The organizational survey I do with clients consists of about 50-55 questions, which will take most people about fifteen minutes to a half-hour to complete. There are both multiple choice and open-ended questions in every section, to allow and encourage additional, anonymous feedback.

I use a virtual survey tool that helps keep data private, and allows users to access the survey anywhere they have internet, including from a cell phone, tablet, or other device.

I also have a (printable or fillable) pdf version of the survey available, free with your purchase of this book[3].

NOTES:

❖ Most people opt for electronic surveys, as they offer the most privacy for the person filling out the survey.

❖ Whenever I do an initial organizational survey, there are certain things I will always dig into. I use almost the exact same survey when I do annual progress reports. I recommend surveying your team at least once a year, to help catch problems when they are still small.

---

3. http://neurodivergentrebel.com/organizational-survey-download/

NOTES (cont...):

❖ Some organizations will need more frequent check-ins, especially, if many risk areas are uncovered through the information gathering process.

Areas to Monitor

Emotional Safety Around NeuroDiversity & Mental Health

Psychological & Emotional Safety enables members of an organization to collaborate freely, share bold and creative ideas, push envelopes, and express themselves openly with one another. When people feel a sense of Emotional Safety, they trust one another and feel safe enough to show up authentically in the workplace.

Questions to ask:

Do you have a stigma-free workplace, where people with invisible differences and mental health conditions feel they can be honest and vulnerable with others inside the organization?

Are people honored and appreciated for their different work and communication styles?

Leadership & Organizational Culture:

Leaders set the example and the culture for an organization.

Organizational culture describes and defines the proper ways in which to behave with an organization.

At the center of an organizations' culture sits its commonly shared values and beliefs that must be supported by planning, careful design, and structure.

Questions to ask:

What are your organizational values? How would you describe your current organizational culture?

Does your organization, especially its leaders, operate with honesty, integrity, trust, accountability, and vulnerability? Do people within the organization generally trust one another?

Accommodations & Accessibility:

Accommodations required will vary depending upon the job tasks and the unique needs of the individual applicant or employee.

Not all NeuroDivergent people will require the same accommodations. If your workplace is set up inclusively, some NeuroDivergent people may not require any accommodations.

It's important to ask:

Is it a fight for people to get what they need to be the best, most effective, version of themselves?

Rules, Policies, & Procedures:

All employees need some form of guidance as a foundation to understand their roles within an organization.

Organizational Rules, Policies, & Procedures help team members understand the values and goals with which they should operate within a workplace, helping to keep everyone in alignment with the organizational matters and practices. However, many policies are not designed with NeuroDivergent minds taken into consideration, and may be (unintentionally) harmful to people whose minds work differently.

Questions to ask:

Is everyone clear on their goals, the organization's vision, and their part in it?

Are your policies unintentionally discriminating against people with invisible differences?

Health Insurance & Benefits:

It's important to offer benefits that employees actually need and find helpful.

Asking your team what benefits they want/if they have what they need in this area can be risky. Are you willing to "put your money where your mouth is" if your employees ask for benefits, you don't currently offer?

For example:

❖ Health Insurance that covers services employees & their family's needs (OT, Speech, etc.).

❖ Flexible Schedules.

❖ PTO & Paid Personal & Sick Time.

❖ Mental Health Days.

❖ Child Care that includes NeuroDivergent Children (since NeuroDivergence often runs in families), including those with multiple disabilities.

Hiring & Recruiting:

NeuroDivergent employees are eagerly entering the workplace, bringing along fresh perspectives and valuable skills. However, while many organizations recognize the need for, and importance of, employing diverse team members, the traditional hiring process can make it difficult for some great workers to get their foot in the door.

Questions to ask:

Is your hiring process unintentionally discriminating against people with invisible differences?

How much weight are you placing on the interview, spoken communication, confidence, and/or likeability when hiring?

Are you giving people the opportunity to showcase their skills vs just talking about their skills? Some NeuroDivergent people may struggle to brag on themselves or tell you what they're good at, but giving them the chance to show you their work can speak for itself.

Onboarding & Training:

Once an organization manages to acquire talent, proper Onboarding & Training become essential for any new employee's success (NeuroDivergent or NeuroTypical).

NeuroDivergent employees may need more support in this initial startup period, and without help, have an increased risk of becoming turnover, especially during the first 90 days of employment.

Questions to ask:

Is your onboarding process providing enough support to people with learning differences? Are you proving the appropriate resources, and teaching people the way they learn?

Are you offering mentors and/or job coaches to new hires and anyone else who would like to have them?

Do you give people enough time to learn everything they need to be successful in their roles (even if some people need more time than others)?

WARNING: Don't ask questions if you are not ready to make actionable change. Creating conversations around organizational issues, making problems known, and then failing to take action can damage your organizational culture, as it will erode trust.

If you are short staffed, spread thin, and worry lots of action items may come from surveying your organization, you may want to break your survey up, focusing on each survey section individually, addressing the problems in each area one by one, before moving on to the next survey section.

Reviewing Feedback from Your Team

Once your organization has completed the organization survey, it's time to review the data or report generated by their responses.

I highly recommend having NeuroDivergent minds involved in both the survey creation as well as the survey report process.

There may be a NeuroDivergent leader on your team eager and willing to step into the role, or you may need to bring in a NeuroDivergent Consultant to help with this step (and the next one).

A well-designed survey will show clearly where your organization is lacking, and will expose many hard truths, in addition to highlighting what you are doing right. However, even a good survey may fail without NeuroDivergent perspectives, as NeuroTypical eyes may miss things in the data that matter to employees whose minds work differently.

Once you have compiled the data, and have a report that protects the anonymity of those surveyed, it's time to share the findings with your team, and discuss results and next steps together.

> **NOTE:** Step 2: Education & Training, can also be "Step 1" if you are not in a place where you are ready to start an organizational survey. However, at minimum, it is important to provide NeuroDiversity training (delivered by a NeuroDivergent team member or outside consultant), and encourage conversations around NeuroDiversity.

Whatever you do, please do not have a NeuroTypical person prepare or deliver training(s) on NeuroDiversity.

Step 2: Education & Training

Though every organization should have the conversation about why NeuroDiversity is important, and how to be supportive allies of NeuroDivergent people, most organizations have never hosted training sessions about NeuroDiversity.

If you haven't already, you will also likely need to find ways to create space for safe dialogue around these topics (NeuroDivergence & Mental Health) within your organization.

Education & training in this area is a must for every organization, especially for business owners and leaders.

Because very few organizations and their leaders currently have an understanding of NeuroDiversity and how this impacts workplaces, Education & Training on the basics of NeuroDiversity (listed as "Step 2" above), may also be used as a "Step 1", to set expectations and prepare your employees for their organizational survey.

Then, depending on your organization's survey results, a customized, more in-depth training (especially for the managers, leaders, trainers, and custodians of people within your organization) may be required.

> **NOTE:** Manager & Leader training should go more deeply into details on how to effectively support, manage, train, and work with your NeuroDivergent hires. Training for HR professionals, recruiters, and trainers should be focused in those specific areas.

Most of what is needed to develop this training can be found within the pages of this book, especially if placed in the hands of someone experienced in designing organizational (or other types of) training.

The **NeuroDiversity 101** or **Intro to NeuroDiversity Training** should teach the following, at minimum:

Define NeuroDiversity and why it matters to organizations, and everyone in them.

Emotional Safety in the Workplace

✤ The need for people to be able to speak up, share struggles, and ask for help.

✤ How pressure to mask and be someone you're not can make work an unsafe place for many NeuroDivergent individuals.

✤ The need all people have to be accepted as they are, plus the importance of NeuroDivergent Authenticity, & the danger of NeuroDivergent Masking & Burnout.

Differences in NeuroDivergent People:

✤ **Communication:** processing differences that impact communication (dyslexia, dyscalculia, audio processing disorder, apraxia of speech, etc.), and how to ensure your employees have the best available tools to use.

> Reminders that spoken communication isn't always the gold standard, but direct, open, & honest communication is priceless.

✤ **Cognitive & organizational differences:** notes about ADHD, and understanding those working with limited working or short term memory, less impulse control, or other cognitive differences.

> Effort to set team members up with the tools for success.

❖ **Sensory differences:** Sensory Processing 101, including:

> What is sensory processing disorder and what are sensory processing differences?

> What is a sensory profile?

> What to do when sensory needs compete.

> Taking an individualized approach to accommodating sensory differences.

❖ NeuroDivergent pace: how NeuroDivergent people's paces can differ from NeuroTypical people's paces, and ways we can be more accommodating with schedules and pacing in the workplace.

Obstacles to Employment

❖ Inaccessible Hiring Process (Recruiting to Onboarding): how traditional interviews often fall short.

> Be sure to list specifics (more in the section of this book titled "Recruiting, Hiring, & Onboarding Neurodivergent Team Members").

❖ Training, Communication, & Unspoken Expectations: how poorly documented expectations, and what's left unsaid can cause unseen harm to people who communicate differently.

> More on this in the section titled "Onboarding: The Value of Proper Training/Education for ALL Team Members".

❖ Accessibility & Accommodations: helping people get their basic needs met (without begging) and creating an environment that empowers people to be the best version of themselves.

> The information needed to craft this portion of the training can be found in the section titled "Accommodating Neurodivergent Employees".

❖ Pressure to conform to NeuroTypical standards: including pressure to mask and blend in, leading to poor mental health, burnout, and lack of Emotional Safety, which leads to increased rates of turnover.

> Information to craft this portion of the training can be found in the sections titled "A Culture that Welcomes Change & New Ways of Thinking & Doing Things" and the section titled "NeuroDivergent Psychological & Emotional Safety".

NOTE: It's important to have a NeuroDivergent person give this training. If you don't have any staff on your team who are able to do this, you may need to source outside help for this piece.

Step 3: Continued Evaluations

The first survey you do with your team will likely unearth many problems you may or may not have been aware of.

Continued evaluations are necessary to gauge progress towards correcting problem areas uncovered in the initial survey.

Reports and data are pointless if action isn't taken on the next steps towards correcting the issues. It is also important to have regular organizational check-ups, to measure progress towards tackling the action items found within the survey data.

You should survey your employees regularly, at least once a year if your organization is doing well (and few risk areas are uncovered during the survey process).

However, if many risk areas are discovered, or there are serious problems in need of attention, it would be good to keep a closer pulse on the organizational culture, surveying the members more frequently (once every 6-9 months).

There is good news! Though creating the first organizational survey was a lot of work, your future surveys can and should be built using the same format or template as the original survey (with room for improvements as needed). In most cases you can re-use the same survey over and over again (once you have created one or tailored it to your organization's unique needs).

These regular check-ins, and continued efforts towards improvements that show measurable results help to keep organizations on track, and foster a sense of accountability. It also provides leaders with a valuable opportunity to follow through on promises, which builds trust (crucial for a healthy organizational culture).

It is likely that many of your organization's problems will be policy related, which is actually good news, because policy is easier to correct than problems with leadership or organizational culture. We will look at some of those common issues in the "" section of this book.

However, we're going to start with the organizational culture information, as although these issues can be more difficult to tackle, they are often the most urgent. Once we've covered this in more depth, we'll move on to information about modifying the physical workspace, and how to put accommodations in place.

As previously mentioned, you are more than welcome to skip around in this book, moving directly to working on the policy related items, if you feel that section calling your name. The most important thing is to start somewhere, and get to a place further down the road towards inclusivity than you were before you started.

If you do choose to skip ahead, please don't forget to come back for the information about organizational culture. The work in that area may be difficult and time-consuming, but it is necessary.

Organizational Culture: It's More than Ping Pong & Beer Taps

While fixing your physical workspace and changing organizational policies are very concrete, simple projects to take on, some of the changes organizations need to make in order to make spaces more accessible to all NeuroDivergent people are a bit more ambiguous.

Organizational culture describes and defines the proper ways in which an employee is expected to behave within an organization. At the center of an organizations' cultures sit its commonly shared values and beliefs (all of which must be supported by planning, careful design, and structure).

A strong culture is a common feature among successful organizations. A company's culture will impact the level of collaboration and productivity that employees demonstrate from day-to-day.

Strong cultures often have fewer disagreements, enhanced trust, cooperation, and are more-efficient when making decisions. People who work within organizations that have strongly defined cultures can easily understand how leaders within the organization would want for them to respond in any given situation.

For an organization's culture to improve organizational performance, its beliefs and values must be widely shared and firmly upheld.

Successful organizations go out of their way to clearly communicate their cultural identities to all members of the team. They are driven by their values and allow their values to determine how the organization will run.

Organizations need to decide which values they want to emphasize, and clearly communicate them to all members of the team. If you don't actively create the culture that you do want within your organization, a culture you don't want can develop organically.

An ineffective or toxic culture can weigh an organization down, leading to poor communication, high turnover, disengaged employees, bad customer relations, and lower profits.

Example of A Strong Culture in Action

Before starting out on my own as an independent NeuroDiversity consultant, I was the VP of Marketing, and Organizational Change Agent, for an amazing consulting firm.

Our culture, at The Firm, was not defined by "perks." We were a values-based organization, meaning we had a culture of shared core values that were clearly outlined and understood by all members of the team.

In that values-driven culture, our clearly defined organization's values created a unified team, with clear direction and goals. This clarity would carry us through both the best and the hardest times.

In the spring of 2020, when COVID-19 came to the United States, many organizations were forced to move to working remotely, something our team had already been doing for the past few months.

The companies whose cultures were built on more shallow office perks struggled, while our culture tied us together.

We didn't have air hockey tables, premium coffee bars, or office bicycles. Instead, our culture was defined by the values and goals that were important to us as a team. As a company, we were always very clear about our goals, intentions, and initiatives. Our achievements were measured in outcomes, not hours worked (which also helped us to attract and retain productive and self-motivated people).

Culture Starts at the Hiring Process

Your organizational culture starts with your hiring process, and the values you look for in the candidates you select: getting the right people in the right seats.

Now more than ever, diversity and inclusion are critical for business success. If you want to recruit people who fit into your company's culture, then you first must define what your culture represents.

When assessing culture fit, it is essential to remember where diversity fits into the equation. Employers that emphasize cultural fit in their recruitment and selection process can be vulnerable to discrimination claims, if the values and culture are set up incorrectly (and many are).

Employers should be aware that certain types of organizational cultures may cause harm to various minority groups, and may even violate anti-discrimination laws.

More and more cases are arising of companies facing lawsuits over employee discrimination disguised as culture fit.

Example of a Discriminatory Culture in Action

I once worked in hiring and recruiting for a company who only hired one type of personality.

Looking back, their checklist of what I was asked to screen for as "proper culture fit" basically translated to "NeuroTypicals only" and "NeuroDivergents need not apply".

Many of the people who were let go at that organization were on performance improvement plans.

Even though I tried to camouflage my weakness, as was expected by my employer, my NeuroDivergent traits often came up on performance reviews, and were noted as things I needed to overcome if I wanted to advance or get raises.

Failure to overcome certain weaknesses, or too much expression of anything others perceived as weaknesses, would be grounds for termination, so I pushed myself to overcome (or hide) any struggles and weaknesses I had.

I didn't know I was Autistic at the time, and remember actively seeking to recruit and hire people who "were not like me", because the people who I related to always were let go.

Many of the people I related to the most were let go for being a "poor culture fit". Why? Because the people who were most like me often didn't understand the unwritten and unspoken rules of our organization's twisted corporate culture, and many struggled with stereotypical ideas of professionalism and dress codes.

Those who failed (and were most like me), did so because they didn't hide their weaknesses and struggles well enough not to have those things used against them by the people in power. This led to them being labeled "problems" by people in charge, for being "too needy", "immature", or "not getting it".

Instead of investing extra time and support in these areas of need, and empowering these team members for success, they were let go without warning.

Behind the scenes, in closed doors, it would be said that they were a "bad culture fit"—something that was never put in writing (probably because of the liability).

While those who "played the games" of office culture well were sometimes let go, they often had a planned exit, and were let go with compassion. Many had help (via referrals) into their next role at another organization in the industry.

Those who had the misfortune of being labeled a "poor culture fit" were the ones let go without warning. They would be completely caught off guard, and far more devastated, by their terminations.

The organization's shallow, personality driven (vs values driven) culture, discriminated against NeuroDivergent people, by valuing NeuroTypical traits and punishing NeuroDivergence, creating a hostile environment for NeuroDivergent employees.

The hostile environment led to increased NeuroDivergent turnover, as well as a decrease in overall NeuroDivergent hiring, as the recruiting team (two NeuroDivergent people) learned that people like them didn't do well within the organization.

What IS a values driven culture?

Having a clearly defined culture, one that's centered on common values and goals (instead of personality, happy hours, and perks), can help prevent discrimination during the hiring process.

Some examples of core values that can help to align people are:

✤ **Respect:** treat others with respect and consideration.

✤ **Servant Leadership:** help first, and serve with gratitude.

✤ **Integrity:** do the right thing.

✤ **Honesty & Trust:** be transparent and honest with each other, to build trust (honesty and trust are built through vulnerability and accountability).

✤ **Accountability:** be willing to take accountability for one's actions and mistakes.

✤ **Responsibility:** embrace opportunities to contribute.

NOTE: Hiring for a value based organizational culture can help future employees to understand and embody your company values, but it doesn't mean dismissing a candidate based on personal beliefs or personal values you may not agree with.

Organizational Evolution

Organizational cultures are constantly evolving, meaning the best employers are those who regularly assess and adjust their organization's culture, helping to ensure that teams and departments can stay engaged, productive, and satisfied with the work they do.

In addition, there are certain types of organizational cultures that, are naturally more inclusive than others. There are also workplace cultures that should be avoided at all costs, as they can be extremely toxic to those whose minds work differently or have other disabilities.

For example, organizational cultures that encourage toxic positivity, and shame people into hiding their weaknesses and struggles can be exceptionally harmful.

I like to call this the "everything is fine culture" where nobody is willing to speak about conflict, problems, or pain.

In these environments, showing signs of weaknesses or needing help is often taboo.

When this type of culture forms, even NeuroTypical and non-disabled team members may be hesitant to speak up when they need help, feel overwhelmed, or are being assigned more than they can realistically handle.

Though "everything's fine cultures" are hard on everyone within an organization, they are most harmful when people need to ask for help.

In cultures that champion self-sufficiency, and discourage people from asking for help, or speaking about struggles and weaknesses, people with disabilities may feel unable to ask for the accommodations they need (and are legally entitled to), because doing so means they may be looked down upon by leadership and peers.

Proper accommodations are often necessary for NeuroDivergent and disabled people to access equitable employment opportunities.

Questions to ask:

✤ Is your organizational culture based on perks and personalities, or is it based on your organizational values and goals?

✤ Does your culture discriminate against NeuroDivergent people by valuing NeuroTypical traits and behavior?

✤ Is your organizational culture saturated with toxic positivity?

✤ Does your culture stigmatize people who ask for help or does it empower them to equip themselves for success?

A Culture that Welcomes Change & New Ways of Thinking & Doing Things

NeuroDivergent people, and those of us who have other disabilities, often need to flex the world and systems around us to fit our needs.

When the systems don't flex, if we are poorly supported, and our needs aren't met, we are more likely to fail, burn out, or leave jobs we could have otherwise done well, if we had been properly supported.

Let's return to Judy Singer for a moment. As I said at the beginning, she was an Autistic sociologist who argued that diverse neurological conditions are the result of normal variations in human brain type.

NeuroDiversity rejects the idea that autism and other neurological processing differences should be cured, and challenges the prevailing views that neurological diversity is inherently something bad.

Unfortunately, most systems in society today, including most workplace systems, have been set up by and for NeuroTypical people (those who are considered to have an "average" or "typical" brain for the time and culture they are currently living in).

These systems are all too often harmful to NeuroDivergent people (those whose brains diverge from what is considered "typical" for the time and culture they are living in) because our needs are not taken into consideration.

Historically, NeuroDivergent people haven't had much opportunity to give input when developing the systems in society, because we are often pathologized, and told that our ways of doing things, thinking, and experiencing the world are wrong, and that we are broken.

Over and over again we are told to try harder to fit ourselves into these broken, outdated systems, instead of flexing the systems, so that we may all evolve and find solutions that work well for everyone.

The systems and structures that favor the majority will often miss or exclude the outliers. This is why it is crucial for organizations and leaders within those organizations to maintain flexibility, and not get stuck in their old ways and systems, as it is highly likely that many of those systems are (often unintentionally) harmful to those who didn't help design it.

If your organization and leadership aren't willing to flex rules or change policies, and are stuck in the "this is the way we've always done things around here" mindset, the changes that must be made won't happen.

NeuroDivergent Psychological & Emotional Safety

Psychological & Emotional Safety enables members of an organization to collaborate freely, share bold and creative ideas, push envelopes, and express themselves openly with one another.

When people feel a sense of **Emotional Safety**, they trust one another and feel safe enough to **show up authentically** in the workplace.

One of the first questions it is important to ask is whether your workplace is one where NeuroDivergent people experience **Emotional Safety**.

❖ Do you have a **stigma-free workplace** where people with invisible differences and mental health conditions feel they can be **honest and vulnerable** with others inside the organization?

❖ Are people honored and appreciated for their different work, thinking, and communication styles?

❖ Do NeuroDivergent people feel they can be open, **OR** are they afraid to speak up because your workplace culture creates pressure for people to mask and hide their struggles and differences?

There are numerous levels of safety (or lack thereof) that NeuroDivergent people might feel when choosing whether to disclose their NeuroDivergence in the workplace.

Ideally, people should feel safe enough to disclose this information openly, without feeling any pressure to hide this fact about themselves, or fear that it will negatively impact their employment.

Sometimes, for personal reasons, a NeuroDivergent Person may not share their NeuroType with others. Unfortunately, being openly NeuroDivergent can bring risks.

For example, if an employee discloses that they are NeuroDivergent, they run the risk of employers, managers and colleagues thinking they are less capable in the workplace, due to their lack of understanding of NeuroDivergent capabilities.

Even more seriously, disclosure outside of work can affect a NeuroDivergent person's entre life. For example, in child custody battles an NeuroDivergent parent's ability to care for their child(ren) may be questioned, even though NeuroDivergent people can be exceptional parents.

Despite the risks, many NeuroDivergent people will at least disclose their NeuroType to select people in an organization, because otherwise it can be difficult to gain accommodation for one's needs. It is the job of the company to ensure they feel safe enough to do so, and carry through on providing the needed accommodations.

If people in your organization haven't disclosed their brain differences, it's important to find out:

❖ If you have NeuroDivergent people on your team or not?

> If not, WHY not???

❖ Are NeuroDivergent people in your organization afraid to share this information with others

> If so, WHY? (Do they have a personal reason outside of work, or are they worried about workplace discrimination?)

❖ Is it possible your workplace is so naturally accommodating to NeuroDivergent minds, that people have not felt the need to bring this information up about themselves in order to get their needs met?

Suggested Actions:

Update your anti-discrimination policy to include NeuroDiversity.

If your organization has a written anti-discrimination policy (you should have this in writing), it would be good to add NeuroDiversity to the list, and make sure everyone on the team knows of this update.

Also, be sure to include this policy in all current and future job listings.

Start, continue, and encourage dialogue and conversations around NeuroDiversity in your workplace.

> **NOTE:** If possible, it's always good to have NeuroDivergent people leading the conversation about NeuroDiversity. This may mean bringing in an outside NeuroDivergent educator, if there are no openly NeuroDivergent team members up to taking on this task.

Encourage conversations around mental health

Remember, NeuroDiversity also includes mental health issues!

When your employees are struggling with their mental health, they should be able to open up and ask for help.

❖ Normalize discussion of mental health by having leadership go first, showing examples of vulnerability by sharing personal stories.

❖ Give employees opportunities to participate in decisions about their own mental health, and issues that have an impact on job stress.

A Culture That Appreciates Everyone's Unique Communication Style

Often things that are binary in the world, are concepts created by people: binary code, binary gender labels, etc.. The truth is, most things in nature occur along spectrums. Humanity itself is a spectrum, just like all types of NeuroDiversity, are spectrums.

Communication Output and Input

A lot of the time, in NeuroDivergent spaces, there is talk about communication output and input. Let's break that down a little.

When talking about communication, it is important to remember that communications come in two parts, communications sent and communications received.

Being NeuroDivergent often can cause differences in how we share, receive, and interpret information that is given to us.

Because human communication is also a spectrum, regardless of NeuroType, it is important for organizations to understand, nurture, and appreciate these communication differences.

Most frequently people talk about outgoing communication, in which speaking, writing, and typing are the most common methods, but there are other communication options such as sign language, letter boards, and ACC, that should be considered and supported.

Communication Output

In workplaces and modern society, spoken speech is often held as the gold standard of communication. However, because, for example, 25-30% of Autistic people can be completely non-speaking, or minimally speaking, this does a huge disservice to NeuroDivergent people who cannot access or struggle with spoken communication.

When working with non-speaking people, it is important to remember those communication channels I mentioned earlier: input and output. Just because someone struggles with the output channel, it doesn't mean they also struggle with the input channel.

Don't ever assume a non-speaker doesn't understand the words coming out of your mouth, just because words aren't coming out of theirs.

Out of those NeuroDivergent people who are able to master spoken speech, many still report having better written communication skills over their spoken communication skills.

For those of us who do better with written communication, writing can allow us to gather and organize thoughts in a more coherent manner.

Now that we've spoken briefly about communication output, what about the processing of input, or incoming communication information?

Communication Input

NeuroDivergent people are more likely to have sensory processing differences that can impact our communication.

NeuroDivergent people who have auditory processing differences and executive functioning differences may struggle to process spoken information.

Those who struggle in these areas may need to get important details and instructions in writing, or another way that's processed visually, with the eyes, instead of auditorily, through the ears. However, this may not always be the case for every NeuroDivergent person you meet.

Many NeuroDivergent people will have more than one NeuroType. For example, Autistic people often have two or three NeuroTypes, in addition to being Autistic. These varied configurations mean no two NeuroDivergent brains will be exactly alike. Even those who share the same NeuroType can have very different experiences and needs.

Autistic people who are also Dyslexic, for example may do better talking through things, and may struggle if you were to provide them too much information in writing or with too many walls of text to try and climb over.

In sharp contrast, Autistics who are hyperlexic, or have audio processing differences may do better if you give them details, tasks, and expectations, in writing.

Communication barriers can create confusion, distrust, and inefficiency, which can lead to frustration for all parties involved, both NeuroDivergent and NeuroTypical.

In order to prevent these communication struggles from impacting your team, it's important to consider the many different factors that can both support and hinder human communication.

No communication style is wrong, but some are looked down upon by societies, more than others.

NeuroDiversity affirming organizations empower everyone in their organization to communicate in the ways that suit them best, and foster appreciation for the differences along the human communication spectrum.

In order to support these differences, one must first understand them.

Communication Differences to Consider

Processing Time

Some people are instantly ready to discuss something that they've just learned, and some will need additional time to process, and adjust, to new information.

There are many reasons someone may need additional time to process, accept, or understand new information, for example:

❖ Cognitive disability.

❖ Previous life experiences that make accepting a specific piece of information difficult.

❖ A mental health condition.

❖ Being naturally more skeptical of new information.

People who live with anxiety will likely tell you that being anxious impacts their communication. If we are feeling anxious or unsafe, we may be closed off or holding back, because we are uncertain whether what we have to say will be accepted.

If we don't have , that also impacts our communication. (More in the section titled "")

Those of us who need more time (for whatever reason) may not be ready to communicate right there at that moment.

If the members of your organization don't feel safe speaking up, for any reason, they're likely holding back and not speaking freely.

Direct & Indirect Communication

Some people people may be painfully honest, calling things as they see it. They may not realize this can be too much, and some people can't handle that.

Often direct communicators are coached to soften their communication, to make it less direct, toning down their intensity, but there's only so much softening someone can do before it becomes restrictive.

People who are fluffy, and soft, and very indirect, aren't asked to flex as often, because our society loves people who can dance around an issue "gracefully". Unfortunately, many of us cannot do this, and find this type of communication confusing.

In addition, direct, open, and honest communication is clear communication.

THE GOAL: Clear communication, so direct and so precise that all questions are answered, and misunderstandings between people with varied NeuroTypes can be avoided. (More in the section titled "")

Amount of Information Needed to Make a Decision

When looking at how people make decisions, some people can easily make quick decisions, and other people will need more time and information before they can commit to a decision or idea.

Additionally, some people are more accepting of new information, while others will naturally be more skeptical.

The accepting people in the team can be a pleasure to work with, because they may not push back on ideas that are presented to them, and are often willing to "go with the flow" or try anything. Accepting people may not worry over how things could go wrong, only thinking about what happens if things go well.

The skeptics are also great to have around, because they tend to be aware of problems and potential ways things can go wrong. When empowered, skeptics are more likely to push back on ideas they feel will lead to poor outcomes.

Some people can find the scrutiny of a skeptic overwhelming, but skeptics don't question things just to be difficult. Many skeptics need to know the "why" behind things and how things work, before they can make accurate decisions and act.

Skeptics are thinking of all the possible outcomes of the situation, and may end up focusing on those that are less than desirable. This can impact a skeptic's communication, because they may need to ask a lot of questions in order to gather the information they need, but will often feel forced into silence.

It can feel like a skeptic is being intentionally difficult, especially if the person talking with a skeptic doesn't understand the need to have as much of the information as possible before making a decision.

Some people, who are more accepting, don't need all of that information in order to be able to make a decision, and those people communicate very differently from someone who needs more details, compared to those who are instantly ready to jump into things.

Both types of people and everyone in between (because these traits happen to different degrees all along the human communication spectrum) are important to an organization or a team's success.

If a team is filled with people who are overly accepting, and nobody is ever willing to question things, it can create frustrating and costly mistakes.

On the opposite side of that coin, if a team is full of skeptics, projects can become bogged down due to over analysis, and the problem of never having "all the information."

Supporting NeuroDiversity, means having a balance of, and empowering, the different types of minds within your organization. Having varied perspectives, experiences, and thinking styles, as well as strengths and weaknesses, means better outcomes, due to more diversity in skill and thought.

Logical or Emotional Decision Making

Emotional Decision Makers

Some of the decision makers on your team will lead with the heart, letting emotions and gut feelings guide their decisions.

These people are often the ones who are quick to think, speak, and act, because they don't need time to weigh out all the pros and cons of a situation. Emotional decision makers trust their gut instincts and are ready to tackle unforeseen problems as they arise, even if they don't know going in what problems might occur.

This is great, when quick decisions must be made. People who are able to quickly lead with their gut can help propel projects and organizations forward. However, more logic focused people may find this too fast, and too dangerous, a way to work.

Logical Decision Makers

The skeptics I mentioned earlier are often more logic focused, and may be able to separate their own feelings from a decision when logic and facts prove their feelings wrong, especially if they understand a situation clearly.

Those logic focused humans may be perceived by emotional decision makers as "cold" or not being sensitive enough to the feelings of others around an issue, because of their ability to detach feelings from their decision-making process.

However, logical decision makers, if empowered to speak up, can play an important role within organizations, alerting others to possible problems and pitfalls, using their logic to prevent mistakes.

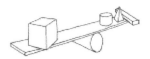

Balance is Important

Just like with people who tend to be more skeptical and people who are more accepting, people who lead with their gut feelings and those who lead with logic can both be valuable members of an organization, especially if there is a reasonable balance between these two thinking types (and both styles are encouraged, valued, and empowered).

Questions to ask:

❖ Is spoken communication considered the "gold standard" within your organization? Are people who communicate in other ways (written, sign, AAC, etc.) empowered, and are their methods of communication equally valued?

❖ Does your organizational culture allow people the time needed to process information? Do people have the space to give input on organizational issues, even if they need more time to think about things?

❖ Are instructions and expectations clear and direct?

❖ Is direct, open, and honest communication welcome within the organization?

❖ Are people who need more information in order to make a decision, empowered to ask questions, or are they scolded for "being difficult"?

❖ Are both logical and emotional decision makers accepted and appreciated within the organization?

A Culture of Appreciation for the Strengths & Weaknesses of ALL Employees

Each person within an organization will operate differently, bringing unique strengths and weaknesses to a team. It is good to have people with varied talents, abilities, NeuroTypes, and backgrounds on a team, this diversity helps with organizational function, planning, and task balancing, especially, if you place together people whose strengths and weaknesses complement one another.

When weaknesses become taboo within a workplace, people are forced do their best to hide their struggles and challenges. Organizations failing to support the different needs and ways in which their team members work means people may be afraid to speak up or ask for the help and resources they need in order to be successful.

NeuroDiversity affirming organizations know how to celebrate, encourage, and empower people's differences. They also have organizational cultures that allow their team members to have human vulnerabilities, and express them freely.

In NeuroDiversity affirming spaces, people aren't asked to "leave pieces of themselves behind" when they come to the office, and the whole person can feel appreciated. This benefits everyone who enters a workspace.

Tips for celebrating differences such as varied work, communication, & thinking styles:

❖ Leadership must set the example that it is okay to have and embrace one's weaknesses by being open with their own struggles (both work and personal).

❖ Help the members of your organization to know, share, and be proud of, their own individual strengths by having roundtable discussions. Ask people to share what they need to be the best version of themselves, for each meeting, for the day, for the week, or just in general.

❖ Encourage regular dialogue about individual communication and processing differences within your organization. Remember to respect and value those differences, being careful not to prioritize one type over others.

> Also encourage people to share what motivates them as well as their pet peeves, what annoys them, and the things people shouldn't do when working with them.

❖ Understand and respect that some employees will flourish with lots of teamwork and social interactions, while others will do better when left to work quietly on their own. Don't shun or punish employees who are less socially inclined or need more solitude.

❖ Remember to schedule ahead, with a clear agenda given, for any meetings or other activities that include someone who needs more processing time, or needs to work up to being social.

A Culture that Values Honesty & Trust

What comes to mind when you hear the phrase "organizational culture"?

Do you think of shallow things, like office bicycles and fully stocked mini bars? **OR** do you think values and ethics?

Too many workplaces these days focus on perks, while forgetting some of the most important workplace values: honesty and trust.

When you came in contact with the word trust above, what was your immediate thought? What does trust mean to YOU?

Is trust knowing that people will do what they say they will do? Is trust knowing the people on your team have your back? Or does trust mean something more or different to you?

Trust can, and must, go deeper, in order for people to feel truly safe within an organization, space, or relationship (personally or professionally). In order to move forward and maximize this type of trust, we must look beyond what workplace trust has meant in the past, in order to help grow something deeper.

Questions to ask when evaluating your organization:

How is conflict handled? Is it productive (does the dialogue end with both parties happy to accept the results, OR do any of them go away frustrated and feeling unheard and unappreciated)?

❖ Can people within the organization openly express their concerns, or disagreements with the group (even with management and team leaders), without fear of rejection, punishment, or retaliation?

❖ Do team members trust that healthy conflict and dialogue will always be encouraged or are people hesitant to speak up when they disagree with ideas or situations?

Do people have enough trust for Emotional Safety? Is vulnerability praised or shamed?

If people feel the urge to act like everything is great, even when the sky is falling, hiding or leaving parts of themselves behind when they come to work, you're already failing.

❖ Can people admit when they are struggling, don't know the answer, or need help, OR is doing so discouraged, instead of encouraged?

❖ Do the leaders go first in admitting when things don't go as planned, they need help, or are struggling, OR do the leaders hide all their weaknesses, problems, and struggles?

❖ Are weaknesses taboo, and people within the organization required to only focus on their strengths, **OR** do people embrace and own all parts of themselves, even areas in which they struggle?

❖ Do you have a "Don't bother me. Figure it out yourself" culture, OR do you have a "there are no silly questions" culture?

What does accountability look like in your organization?

Too often we only think of leadership holding team members accountable, but this is only one side of the coin.

✤ Can team members trust leadership enough to hold them accountable, allowing team members enough trust that they can effectively manage up?

✤ Do people within the organization hold themselves and each other accountable for doing the things they say they will do by when? Is there peer to peer accountability?

Leadership Drives Culture

"Leaders are the ones who dare to go first, to put themselves at personal risk to open a path for others to follow." - Simon Sinek.

Does your organizational leadership have flexibility, or are they stuck in their old ways & systems?

Leaders can help to motivate and drive an organization forward, or they can slow down its progress, demoralizing team members and driving an organizations' culture into the ground.

Meaningful trust from leadership is essential for an organization to be NeuroDiversity affirming.

Trust and respect are earned, and leaders who are not trustworthy, don't do what they say they will do, or stifle their direct reports, can ruin an organization.

Often, when leaders hear the words trust, they immediately think it's about "trusting employees to do work even if they are unsupervised". Some managers may feel as if they simply can't trust some team members to work without their watchful eye, which may be true for some team members.

Some people may want, need, and thrive with more supervision, however having too much supervision, or being micromanaged, can create tension and break trust.

Being micromanaged can cause feelings of frustration and inadequacy, especially if a managers' hovering eyes are lingering when a team member is doing work they don't need help with. Constant corrections, and insertions of "I would do it this way" or "are you sure you did X, Y, or Z" can begin to create feelings of self-doubt and distrust.

If you are micromanaging people you work with, they may feel as if you don't trust them, their judgements, or ability to do quality work—even if that's not your intention.

Trust is a type of mutual respect between two parties. If the people who report to you don't feel you trust them, it will be impossible for them to trust you.

REMINDERS FOR LEADERS

The leader must go first. People within organizations will often look to managers and leadership as an example of how they should model their own behaviors within an organization.

For example, if a leader is working around the clock, and responding to email after hours, employees may see that and feel pressured to work after hours too, even if your organizational policy warns against working outside of office hours.

Similarly, if a leader hides all their weaknesses, cannot be vulnerable, and regularly breaks promises, the people who report to that leader may follow that lead and are likely to act in a similar way. Not only that, but they will also distrust that leader, and possibly each other, thus creating an even more damaged team relationship.

Action Items for Leaders

❖ Leaders must be willing to model vulnerability for those they lead by asking for help and input, and being vulnerable by sharing when they are struggling or uncertain, so that team members know vulnerability and asking for help are not only okay, but encouraged.

❖ Leaders must be trustworthy, doing what they say they will do by when they say they will do it. They must hold themselves accountable when they make mistakes, owning up to any missed expectations and promises.

✤ Leaders must be open to having their direct reports managing up. Accountability must go in all directions, not only from leader to team member, but also from peer to peer, and from team member back up to leadership. Every single team member, regardless of role, should feel safe holding all other members of the organization accountable.

Deep, Meaningful, Organizational Trust

Organizations that lack deep, meaningful, trust will have more unproductive conflicts; the type of conflict that creates tension without results, causing increased aggravation for all parties involved.

In addition, when trust is weak in any relationship, professional or personal, people may not feel safe enough to take risks, think outside the box, or let their more vulnerable parts show.

Baring the most vulnerable parts of yourself isn't something most people do with people they don't trust or if they are feeling unsafe.

For those with invisible disabilities, sharing our hidden struggles and weaknesses can be a risk many of us can't or won't take, especially if we don't trust that sharing this information with others will be safe, and won't lead to discrimination, resentment, and stigmatization.

A Culture that Embraces Vulnerability

Real bravery isn't repressing and hiding our emotions. Despite what we're often taught, being vulnerable requires bravery. It takes real courage to bear your soul to the world, knowing that you may be judged harshly, scolded, or even shunned for it.

Vulnerability can be scary, but is often necessary when expressing our wants and needs, especially if we feel other people may judge, or misunderstand us for expressing those needs. This is especially true, for those with invisible differences, such as NeuroDivergence or other marginalized human variety.

Showing vulnerability in unsafe situations can be dangerous. Being mocked, exploited, or scolded for expressing vulnerability is traumatic, and many of us have been trained, teased, punished, scolded, and otherwise discouraged from admitting our weaknesses, speaking up when we're uncomfortable, or asking for help.

For people to be vulnerable, they must first feel safe. Therefore, it is imperative that organizations create space for open and honest conversations, where team members have the Emotional Safety they need in order to be vulnerable.

I'll say this again because it always bears repeating: team members will often mimic behaviors that are modeled by their leaders.

Leaders set the tone

In order to grow a culture of vulnerability-based trust, leaders must go first and be open and honest when sensitive topics arise.

Both leaders and team members should be encouraged to be open and honest with their mistakes, weaknesses, failures, and need for help.

If leaders cannot be vulnerable and admit struggles, problems, and worries, that behavior will be mirrored by those who report to them. This can create a culture where weakness and asking for help are taboo, shutting down teamwork and collaboration.

Team members with invisible differences or mental health struggles may not feel safe enough to speak up when they are struggling and ask for help, especially if everyone around them is hiding their weaknesses behind walls of false strength.

Question to ask:

Is your corporate culture one where NeuroDivergent people feel a need to hide their struggles, or does the organizational culture create an empowering environment for NeuroDivergent team members?

Putting it into practice

A good exercise, that can help to build vulnerability and open discussions around mental health and NeuroDiversity in the workplace, is simply to have regular check-ins with team members on how they are doing from day-to-day.

To encourage Emotional Safety, have your team leaders go first, sharing their own vulnerabilities, modeling that doing so is welcomed, and encouraged within your organization.

If your organization (or individual teams within larger organizations) has a daily team Sync Up Meeting (a quick 5–15-minute meeting, depending on the size of the team), where employees each share about their day, projects, and current workload, make an effort to work vulnerability into those meetings.

It can also be helpful to use these meetings as a time where people can request help from their team members on their current projects if needed. This encourages collaboration and normalized speaking up and asking for help.

If you don't have a daily team check-in, where team members gain alignment and sync up each day, it may be something to strongly consider.

REMEMBER:

Sync Up Meetings are FAST. They're not meant to drag on and on.

Sync Up Meetings should be close to the beginning of every work day or shift.

For a Sync Up Meeting, each person quickly shares, in under a minute, 3 things:

1. **How they are doing that day & what's going on in their life.**

Ask each leader and team member to share how they are feeling, using a one to ten scale (one being horrible and ten being AMAZING). Are they feeling great, or are they not the best version of themselves that day because of something they're struggling with in their personal life?

> **NOTE:** Asking people to leave their personal life at the door, is asking them to leave their humanity behind.

If someone is worried about a loved one passing away, has lost a loved one, or about some other major life event, it is cruel and unrealistic to expect them to perform as well as they can on their very best day.

When people can admit that they're not at their best, or that they need help with something required of them, they are empowered to get the help they need. If people pretend they're okay when they're not, it holds them back because the help they need won't be provided.

1.   **What their schedule for the day looks like.**

Sharing things like what they are working on that day, if they're available to help others, or if they need help themselves.

> **Also**, it's good to share if they will be out of the office, or leaving at a certain time.

1.   **Anything they need from the team.**

What does each person need to be their best, most effective, versions of themself?

> **It can vary from day-to-day.** This is a time to state needs, whether it's to be left alone to do quiet work, help brainstorming, or guidance on a project.

Sync Up Meetings are great, because they can help encourage open discussions around mental health and NeuroDiversity. In addition, they serve as a space where team members can ask for, and offer to help, one another.

These meetings can also be a driver of positive and nurturing organizational cultures, based on values over hollow perks (like mini bars), because team members are understanding, and empathizing with, one another.

A Culture of Accountability & Trust

Accountability is needed to build trust in both professional and personal relationships, and is foundational in helping teams work more effectively together.

Are members of your team routinely breaking promises and missing deadlines? Do your leaders regularly feel they must micromanage those they lead, nagging team members for updates and interfering where they aren't required?

If these scenarios sound familiar, your organization may have a problem with accountability, emotional safety, and trust.

Accountability, emotional safety, and trust are related and impact one another. They are also three of the most important values for an organization to have, if they want to include those with invisible differences.

Notes about Accountability & Trust:

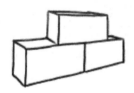

People must feel safe (and encouraged) to ask for help and admit struggles when needed.

Trust and emotional (or psychological) safety are the building blocks upon which accountability rests. If you lack either or both of these pillars, team members won't feel safe and open, and they may also struggle to take ownership when problems arise or projects are off track for fear of reprisal.

Accountability and trust are values that take time to grow. We can cultivate accountability and trust through regular progress reports, open and honest communication, and by creating a space where people are empowered to share when they need help, or are struggling (personally or professionally).

Implementation:

Strongly recommended: Daily, weekly, or twice per week check-ins, using the Sync Up model, where teammates share important updates regarding their projects and their needs with the rest of the team.

Unclear expectations and a lack of specificity are enemies of accountability.

These check-ins are an opportunity for team members to ask other team members or leaders for help or resources they may need, and is also a great time for each team member to share how they're doing (including if they're feeling great, are available to help others, are currently overwhelmed, or are not currently the best version of themselves).

> **NOTE:** If someone discloses that they need help, or are at risk of falling behind on a project, it is important not to scold them. Remember, this isn't something they're doing on purpose. Instead, support that team member by offering

help, asking what they need, and checking if any obstacles to their project can be removed by other team members or organizational leadership.

Tip: To prevent and reduce confusion, make plans and instructions as clear and precise as possible.

Be sure to clearly define the following:

❖ Who (roles and responsibilities).

❖ What (needs to be done).

❖ How (any specifics).

❖ When (a clearly defined deadline known and understood by all).

Policy Related: Accommodating Neurodivergent Employees

Defining Diversity & Inclusion

Diversity and inclusion are two related concepts that must work together for organizations to be successful.

Diversity relates to the makeup of an organization's people—their most valuable resource—while inclusion reflects how the organization values and supports and engages them.

An inclusive workplace is one in which all employees have a voice, whilst feeling respected and valued.

When we change the workspace to accommodate all NeuroDivergent employees, we are also making the workplace more inclusive and better for everyone, including NeuroTypicals. A truly inclusive workplace creates and empowers each employee to reach their full potential, bringing their best self to work.

Not only is inclusion the right thing to do, it's actually better for the bottom line. A 2019 Deloitte LLP study found that inclusive organizations are eight times more likely to achieve better business outcomes, six times more likely to be innovative, and twice as likely to meet or exceed financial targets[1].

Inclusion is a long-term commitment, and will require continuous work requiring you to remain flexible. This is why continued evaluations, and a culture of open and honest feedback and communication across all levels of the organization are necessary. You

---

1. https://www2.deloitte.com/content/dam/insights/us/articles/4209_Diversity-and-inclusion-revolution/DI_Diversity-and-inclusion-revolution.pdf

want to catch problems before they are out of control, and gently steer your organization into the future.

Thinking About Accommodations Differently

Different people within an organization will find different aspects of their work motivating/stressful.

NeuroDivergent people have different skills and weaknesses from their NeuroTypical peers, and may struggle with things that seem simple to others, while excelling at tasks that can seem to be more complicated to NeuroTypical onlookers. True workplace NeuroDiversity takes advantage of this, instead of punishing it, by pairing people with different skills and weaknesses together.

Instead of berating employees for their shortcomings, forcing them to only focus on overcoming their perceived weaknesses, a NeuroDiversity based model empowers the members of your organization to come in and focus on what they are good at.

When people are allowed to play to their strengths in the workplace, they come to work eager to do work that they enjoy, and show up ready to do their best work.

Example of Workplace NeuroDiversity Inclusion in Action

As I mentioned in the , I didn't know I was Autistic until I was almost thirty years old. Before I was diagnosed and had a vocabulary around my needs and a good understanding of what Autism was and how that related to me, I could not adequately advocate for my needs within the workplace, or even describe to others what they were.

I didn't understand how my NeuroDivergence impacted certain areas in my life (why some things that came naturally to my peers seemed difficult or nearly impossible for me).

I am also Hyperlexic (in my case this is related to being Autistic).

Because of how my brain processes and interprets information, I don't read phonetically, as many people do. Each word is its own picture. Hyperlexia also means my brain is lighting fast when interpreting written text.

Instead of reading word for word, I digest paragraphs at a time. I've tried to slow myself down, but for some reason, my brain compiles information and corrects typos so quickly that I often don't see them even if they're right in front of me.

NeuroDivergence isn't an excuse. It's an explanation. With this skill of lightning fast reading, comes the struggle with accuracy and proofreading.

It's a difference in my skillset, thanks to my NeuroDivergent brain, which is often contrasted to the NeuroTypical expectation to slow down and see typos in text.

However, not all NeuroDivergent people have the same strengths or difficulties. Though some experiences are common, each NeuroDivergent person is unique. A dyslexic person may also have typos in their work, for example, but for different reasons.

There are also NeuroDivergent people whose ability to spot inconsistencies, may cause them to be a fantastic proofreader. I, personally, would love to have this skill, but do not. I have even taken proofreading classes to try and help myself in this area, with no luck. My brain just cannot process text that way.

Proofreading has been my biggest enemy. I am not the right person to proofread things that must be accurate, because I will see the wider meaning, and miss the typos.

Not being able to catch typos was a sticking point for one of my previous employers, who even expected internal emails, chats, and communications to be typo-free. Neither the employer nor I knew that I had a learning difference.

It was put on my performance review multiple times because I "had a typo in an internal email", and managers chastised me in our one to one meetings, saying that I "couldn't be trusted with emailing clients if I had typos on internal communications."

I was scolded so much for this part of my disability that I still have extreme anxiety when sending emails.

Despite my best efforts, and extreme desire to be a good proofreader, because of the configuration of my brain, it's not a skill that I will ever master.

As a perfectionist (a strength or weakness depending on what I'm trying to do), doing my best, and trying hard to meet expectations that had been placed upon me, the constant critique of something I couldn't control ate at me on the inside.

I developed severe anxiety around written communication and emails (a method that had always been accessible to me before).

I would overthink every aspect of every email I sent, and often retract them after sending to re-check for typos, sometimes multiple times. Will I miss something? Is there a mistake I am not seeing?

Send. Retract. Send. Retract. Send one last time.

Years, and jobs later, I would find myself stuck in a cycle of re-reading emails 10-15 times, looking for typos, before finally sending them, and retracting them several more times to check for typos again, before finally sending...and then checking the outbox one last time for typos, terrified I'd find a letter or number out of place.

The panic I would feel before and after hitting send on any email, text message, or social media post was intensely nauseating, causing me to avoid communicating in the way people understand me best.

It would take an employer with a more compassionate, NeuroDiversity affirming approach to snap me out of the overwhelming fear and shame.

I still feel the effects of the extreme self doubt that was placed in me years ago. Even now, my confidence in my writing ability remains shaken, despite the kind way my most recent employer handled this part of my disability.

The anxiety forced on me by that former employer has affected everything since. This is the result of a workplace that demanded conformity to a NeuroTypical culture.

What I needed to learn was that although I cannot see typos and am not a great proofreader, I CAN work with someone who has this skill, to support me in this area of weakness.

My next employer did a better job of understanding and supporting this need I had, and used what they learned from supporting my needs as an opportunity to support anyone else who may have had a similar experience within our organization.

A great solution that worked well with a more inclusive employer, was just to have a two sets of eyes rule.

This rule was that any external or client-facing document must be passed through one of the team's designated proofreaders (people who excelled in the area that I lacked) before being sent to the client.

In the more inclusive company, all team members were permitted and encouraged to request a second set of eyes for important emails before sending them. More importantly, nobody ever mentioned typos on internal emails (or even external emails), if they weren't serious.

The other very important piece of the two sets of eyes policy was that it was a great example of honoring NeuroDiversity in the workplace.

Remember: NeuroDiversity includes ALL brains, NeuroDivergent AND NeuroTypical.

One reason the second set of eyes policy worked out so well was because the rule applied to everyone on the team, not just the

NeuroDivergent team members, to avoid segregating or singling anyone out.

In addition, everyone on the team was given access to a Grammarly Premium subscription, for use on our laptops and cell phones.

The two sets of eyes rule also meant that documents and emails received by clients, having gone through someone with proofreading as a strength, were better prepared, thus lifting the company as a whole.

In truly NeuroInclusive organizations, it doesn't matter that a few employees with skills in other areas are weak at a common skill like proofreading, because we are able to work with people whose strengths and weaknesses are different from one another. In fact, that's the beauty of NeuroDiversity: everybody has their weaknesses covered by someone from whom they are strengths, and can aid others whose weaknesses lie in their strengths.

The goal of your NeuroDiversity initiative should be to create a genuinely inclusive workplace that doesn't force NeuroDivergent team members into separate systems. I challenge you to examine if your policies are creating **inclusion or segregation**.

Don't Depend on Disclosures & Separate Pipelines

People should be able to succeed in your workplace even if they don't know they are NeuroDivergent (especially since there are many people out there who have no idea).

These employees are less likely to speak up and ask for help, because they may not fully understand their needs, may have had trouble explaining them, or have struggled in getting people to take them seriously in the past.

Silent turnover is a significant expense for businesses when skilled, devoted, employees quietly move on without asking for help.

In addition, even if your employees know they are Neurodivergent, they may not feel comfortable sharing this information with you.

Unfortunately, many of us have had bad experiences with disclosure in the past. Depending on the industry, organization, or even the individual manager, sharing their NeuroDivergent diagnosis can bring discrimination, and may even be career limiting.

We shouldn't have to disclose our NeuroType to have our needs met and respected. Policies and procedures can be set up to take everyone in the organization into account, but some flexibility is needed.

It's essential to be open to changing how we do things instead of getting stuck because "that's just the way we've always done things around here."

If an employee comes to you their employer, and says "I'm working on this project, but need [fill in the blank] to do my job better, you'd typically oblige them if their request is within reason and won't cause harm to the business, especially if it will empower them to do their job more effectively. Wouldn't you? If not...ask yourself why not?

It is important not to be closed off to these types of requests, even if we don't personally understand the need.

Example of NeuroDiversity in Action

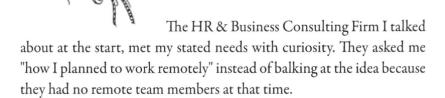

The HR & Business Consulting Firm I talked about at the start, met my stated needs with curiosity. They asked me "how I planned to work remotely" instead of balking at the idea because they had no remote team members at that time.

I started out as the organization's first remote employee, but eventually, the entire team would end up working remotely, and in the fall of 2019, before COVID hit the United States the following spring, we would turn in the keys to our physical office, saving money on office space and ensuring we were ahead of the game when the US went into lockdown a few months later.

Because the employer had asked WHY instead of saying NO, and committed to trying something new, we were lucky enough to have systems in place for remote working already when doing so became mandatory very suddenly in 2020.

While other businesses were struggling to figure out how their teams could transition to remote work, we continued to operate from the safety of our homes, moving our few in-person meetings to virtual.

It turned out that accommodating me, the team's first openly NeuroDivergent employee, with the ability to work remotely (then opening the option anyone else who wanted to work remotely if their job functions allowed it) ended with everyone working remotely, and our company saving a lot of money that would have been completely wasted on unusable office space during the lockdown.

Workplace Adjustments

NeuroDivergent employees must be permitted to **adapt the systems and spaces around them**, in order to work equitably in spaces that weren't designed with their needs in mind.

Reasonable accommodations are adjustments to a workplace environment, policy, or procedure, that enables people with disabilities and varied NeuroTypes to perform their job tasks efficiently and productively.

These adjustments help people to get their basic needs met, create an environment that empowers people to be the best version of themselves, and **are essential** to allowing employees with disabilities and varied NeuroTypes to be able to **thrive in the workplace**.

Accommodations will vary depending upon the job tasks and the **unique needs** of the individual applicant or employee.

For organizations wanting to employ those with invisible and visible disabilities, **Accommodations & Accessibility** are essential tools for employee **retention and advancement**.

NOTE: Not all NeuroDivergent people (even two people with the same NeuroType) will require the same accommodation. Also, if your **workplace is set up inclusively**, some NeuroDivergent people may not require any accommodation.

Protected By Law

By law, in most countries, people with disabilities are legally protected and entitled to reasonable accommodations upon request, and an employer is required to make a reasonable accommodation to a known disability of a qualified applicant or employee if it would not impose an "undue hardship" on the operation of the employer's business[2].

The phrase "known disability" here matters in the case of NeuroDivergence especially, because many of us may already be in the workplace, without knowing that our minds are, in fact, different.

In some parts of the world, adult diagnosis may be unavailable, or waitlists can be years long. Poverty, age, gender, and minority status can also impact a person's ability to receive a medical diagnosis.

Because of these inequities in the diagnostic process (that often have the most impact on NeuroDivergent people who are multiply-marginalized), requiring medical proof for accommodations can leave many NeuroDivergent employees without proper support.

Disability laws are in place to be the **bare minimum level of support** and anything less is considered criminal.

Serious Questions to Ask

✤ Are you really okay with settling for the bare minimum when supporting your employees?

---

2. https://www.eeoc.gov/laws/guidance/fact-sheet-disability-discrimination

❖ You followed the law and covered your back, but could you have done more?

❖ Are you okay with your half-assed disability inclusion efforts?

❖ Do you care if your employees feel as if they matter to you?

Sixty one million adults in the United States alone have a disability. That means twenty six percent (one in 4) of adults in the United States have some form of disability[3]. If you're doing just the bare minimum in supporting one in four of your employees, it is likely that one in four of your employees don't feel very appreciated, or feel as if their needs don't matter to your organization.

Not an Afterthought

Truly inclusive systems are designed to work with everyone's needs taken into account, and accessibility isn't an afterthought.

Truly inclusive systems include people with disabilities and invisible differences (as more than token hires and quota meeting). They don't make us go through separate pipelines and gatekeepers, to gain access to the support we need to be successful.

When an employee comes to you, and lets you know that there is something that they need in order to do their job more effectively, as long as there is no harm that would come to the organization by providing this support, why not give them what they ask for, and empower them to do their job well?

---

3. https://www.cdc.gov/ncbddd/disabilityandhealth/infographic-disability-impacts-all.html

Let team members work with headphones, turn off lights, or modify their schedule to start earlier, later, or include movement breaks. Give employees tools and support, like Grammarly, organization programs, job coaches, or extra time with a mentor if they request it.

It is important to be willing to meet people where they are with their individual human needs, and try to stay flexible.

In addition, organizations should frequently examine, update, and change organizational rules, policies, and procedures, especially when they find out something they've been doing is causing harm.

Differences in NeuroDivergent People to Accommodate

In order to be proactive, instead of reactive, you need to understand and take the invisible differences that NeuroDivergent people have into account.

What are some of these differences, and what actions can you take, preemptively, to prevent the exclusion of NeuroDivergent employees?

NeuroDivergent people's differences are cognitive, invisible, and impact the way we interpret the world, process information, and interact with others.

Communication Differences

When looking at communication, NeuroDivergence can impact the way we interpret and share information in many ways.

NeuroDivergent people's communication differences can range from being very talkative (seeming to not know when to stop talking), to non-speaking, and using AAC, typing, or sign language to communicate. Spoken communication isn't always the gold standard with NeuroDivergent brains.

Some of us may stutter, have difficulty moderating our indoor/outdoor voices, or have moments where we cannot make the right, or any, words come out.

We may need or prefer written communications over spoken, or require more time to gather our thoughts. Some of us may ramble off long streams of information, without pausing to give others a chance to jump in.

Autistic people, specifically, can also tend to be VERY direct.

We can struggle to read body language and facial expressions, or may find eye-contact uncomfortable and unnerving.

Some NeuroDivergent people may be visual thinkers which can cause problems and confusion in translation when people talking to us causes the wrong mental pictures to be painted OR if we struggle explaining what it is we are visualizing.

This is one reason some of us tend to take things literally, because of the literal pictures we see when people are communicating with us.

Though there are some NeuroDivergents who seem to never stop talking, there are also NeuroDivergent people who do not speak with their mouths at all, or have very limited mouth speech.

This is because being NeuroDivergent can often cause movement differences, where our motor control may be enhanced or reduced, such as with dyspraxia and apraxia.

Apraxia of speech does not allow the translation of speech to the muscles of the mouth. I repeat: this is a muscle control issue NOT a comprehension issue. This does not mean these NeuroDivergent people do not understand speech or language or that they have nothing to say.

Non-speaking NeuroDivergent people have a LOT to say, if we take the time to listen to them.

These NeuroDivergent people may use AAC devices, sometimes on a tablet, laptop, or phone, to read off text as their voice **OR** may depend on written communication over communicating with spoken words.

Some NeuroDivergent people never speak with their mouths, and even those of us who do speak this way, can be situationally limited in this area.

For example, I lose the ability to speak if I am under extreme distress, and can become trapped inside myself, screaming on the inside, knowing EXACTLY what I wanted to say, but not being able to physically move my mouth to make the words come out.

Scrambled Communications

Our communications can be scrambled both on the way in, and on the way out.

Because of this, you may need to write or type to communicate best with some NeuroDivergent people, if they struggle to process and decode spoken language.

NeuroDivergent people with Audio Processing Differences, may struggle to process spoken speech accurately (even if we speak fluently with our mouths). Some NeuroDivergent people may struggle to understand people well enough to communicate effectively in loud or busy environments, because the business, movements, and sounds overwhelm them.

It is an incredibly frustrating feeling, wanting to communicate and not being able to, or not being heard. Imagine being brushed off, or assumed to be unintelligent, just because your communication needs differ from those of most NeuroTypical people. Now imagine someone taking the time to listen, instead. You should always try to be the second person.

> **DON'T FORGET:** While some people prefer and need written communications, there are also NeuroDivergent people who may need and prefer spoken communications. For example: the dyslexic person, or the ADHDer, who doesn't do well when faced with a wall of text.

Regardless of how we communicate (with our mouths or not), direct, open, and honest communication is one of the best accommodations for NeuroDivergent people. Our individual communication needs will determine how that communication is handed down.

A lot of things NeuroDivergent people need are things everyone can appreciate and benefit from. This is another reason why creating inclusive workplaces benefits everyone within an organization.

What is your organization currently doing to support people with varied communication needs?

Some important questions to ask yourself, as you think about the way communication is handled moving forward:

❖ Are people with varied communication needs valued and respected, beyond just written or spoken communication?

❖ Are you making sure everyone who wants to share is given the chance to do so, or are you letting the more outgoing people dominate conversations, speaking over those who are more reserved?

❖ Do you also respect people who are socially anxious, or are unsure, or nervous at the idea of speaking up in a room full of people?

❖ Some people are quick to speak, needing little time to think over their responses, but other people may need more time. Is there space for these team members to give input at a later time if needed?

Are you facilitating a mindset that truly values these differences in the human communication spectrum, or are you excluding people with differing communication needs?

❖ Are your managers and leaders giving directions and instructions in multiple ways, for example: making a request out loud, then following up with details/instructions in writing?

❖ Do people have the time, and feel safe, to ask questions and clarify things (without being shamed) if they are confused about something?

❖ Are the people planning organizational meetings and functions taking these communication differences into account when they are planning company gatherings?

❖ Do you currently offer transcriptions, closed captioning, and other meeting summary documents, with all action items, expectations, assignments, and deadlines outlined in a clear way (so the people assigned to tasks have a record of these expectations for future reference)?

Cognitive & Organizational Differences

Some NeuroDivergent people may not have the ability to organize and track tasks internally, instead needing to organize themselves externally using paper, the cloud, or some other tool.

Because some of us have limited access to our working or short term memory, it can be helpful to give information in multiple ways. For example, if requesting someone to help you with a task or giving directions, a good practice is to make the request out loud, but also offer to give directions in writing or allow the person time to make their own notes. Making these options available is important in particular if you're asking someone to do a task with multiple steps: this way they won't have to worry about forgetting any of the important information.

If giving directions out loud, it is also good practice to have the person repeat back to you what they understood about your instructions. This works both ways as well: when receiving directions, you can be the one to repeat back your understanding of the instructions you've been given. This way any misunderstandings can be cleared up immediately, saving time and frustration on all sides.

Some additional considerations when creating documents and sharing visuals and text could be:

✤ All organizational rules, policies, and procedures, being clearly outlined in writing and available to every single member of the organization for easy reference.

✤ When giving directions in writing, make extra effort to clearly organize text, and avoid text walls (which some people may struggle with), by using numbered lists, bullet points, boxes, and clean, uncluttered, design choices.

✤ Be mindful of the fonts, colors, and arrangements of text, to avoid visual clutter or overload. For example, bright colors (even bright white) can be painful or distracting; text that doesn't have enough contrast from the background can be hard to read; and small fonts and poor line spacing can also cause trouble for some readers.

✤ Icons and visual reminders can also be helpful, but don't forget to create image descriptions and alt text for those with visual differences that require them.

Sensory Differences

It is important to consider people's sensory, communication, and processing differences when designing spaces and holding meetings (in person or virtual), and one to one settings.

In your work with NeuroDivergent populations, the first, and often easiest, accommodations you can make are going to be changes to the physical sensory environment.

NeuroDivergent people can have sensory processing differences, sometimes referred to as a sensory processing disorder, which causes problems in our ability to live and function in the current modern-day world, that wasn't designed with our needs in mind.

NeuroDivergent sensory profile ranges often tend to be in the extreme ends of things. In certain areas of our sensory profile, we will usually be over- or under-sensitive when compared to NeuroTypical people.

NOTE: Though doing so is unfair, NeuroDivergent people are constantly compared to what's considered "typical" for nonNeuroDivergent (or NeuroTypical people) - despite the fact that "typical" is relative and constantly changing, depending on the group of people you're surrounded by, your geographical location, and many other fluid factors.

What is a Sensory Profile?

Each and every human being, NeuroDivergent or NeuroTypical, has their own unique sensory profile. This can vary greatly from person to person. Even two people with the same NeuroType can have very different sensory experiences and profiles.

I find it helps to think of sensory processing, and people's individual sensory profiles, as a DJ's soundboard, with all the sliders that can go up or down.

There is an average range in the middle (where non-autistics and NeuroTypicals tend to sit). NeuroDivergent people tend to slide up or down from those averages.

Then sliders can be adjusted for each of the senses – sight, smell, touch, vision, taste, balance, how well you feel your body in space.

My Sensory Profile?

If we take my specific personal sensory profile, for example:

❖ Fluorescent lighting makes me physically ill. I can have seizures and migraines from them.

❖ I can hear and am bothered by sounds that other people often don't even notice.

❖ I get cold VERY easily, and can't stand the sensation of moving air on my arms.

❖ There are also certain fabrics and textures of clothing that feel like fire ants biting my skin.

❖ I also have audio processing difficulties that can cause me to mishear words.

❖ My balance on my two feet isn't the best, and I struggle with spatial awareness and motor planning, so I'm always bumping into walls and tables. This means driving is also difficult for me.

Because of this, my sensory environment is always top of mind. I'm only really physically comfortable when I have almost complete control over my environment/situation.

I can come off as overly controlling sometimes, due to the amount of control I need in my life, so it's important that the people around me are aware, and understanding, of my needs.

How can you give some of the needed control back to your NeuroDivergent and sensory sensitive coworkers?

Think carefully about the spaces around you, both the office spaces you work in and the stores and public spaces you enter.

❖ Do the rooms echo?

❖ Are the lights and AC units bright or loud?

❖ Are there a lot of people talking at once or are there lots of competing types of sounds (music, plates, footsteps, phones, machines, etc.)?

❖ Do you have (or can you create) a quiet, sensory friendly space, free of artificial/bright lights, away from loud or sudden noises, and smells?

Often it can be something as simple as moving a meeting somewhere quieter, so people can engage more easily, or turning off the lights in one half of a meeting room or office space so people can work in whichever lighting makes them most comfortable.

Competing Sensory Needs

What about when people's sensory needs are in conflict with one another?

Sensory processing differences aren't uniform and every single human being has unique sensory needs (whether they are NeuroDivergent or NeuroTypical).

One NeuroDivergent person's idea of pure joy may be torture for the next NeuroDivergent.

Sensory Differences in Action

For example, I'm very sensitive to cold, but my NeuroDivergent partner is more sensitive to heat. I'm also light sensitive and my partner LOVES (and sometimes needs) big, bright, annoying, lights that hurt my eyes.

This makes life in our home very interesting...and is a constant struggle.

My number one enemy is bright, blue fluorescent lighting BUT other people NEED bright lights to read.

Some NeuroDivergent people are not sensitive to sensory experiences at all.

It can vary greatly from person to person, and though there are some things you can do in advance to make your environments more welcoming for people of varied sensory profiles, because we are all individuals you should ensure you build sensory profiles for all employees, and do what you can to accommodate them.

What does this type of accommodation look like?

❖ Lighting: you can do simple things, like turn off lights. You can also allow people to put a lamp on their desk, if they need more light in a room.

❖ Sound: if it's too loud (or quiet) for someone, you can allow them to move to another location which is more comfortable. You can also close doors which are open to noisier places, and allow people to work whilst wearing headphones.

❖ Smell: don't put people who are sensitive to smells near areas with strong smells such as bathrooms, kitchens or break rooms. Allow them to open a window to allow fresh air flow, use a desk air freshener, and increase air purification systems (especially if people have allergies).

MOST IMPORTANTLY: Make a point to let people around you know that if they are uncomfortable, you want them to speak up. Make sure that they know you are looking out for their needs, and help them get used to speaking up and advocating for themselves around you and in your workplace.

Many NeuroDivergent people won't be used to that, or may have experienced workplaces where their needs were not respected in the past. Often they will have had experiences that show them the opposite, so may need some help and gentle coaxing at first.

If you have not already fixed your organization's sensory environment and aren't actively accommodating sensory processing differences, it is likely your organization is experiencing the silent (and costly) loss of NeuroDivergent sensory sensitive people who feel unsupported and undervalued.

The helpful Sensory Friendly Space Guide on the following pages can help you to evaluate the spaces around you.

Sensory Friendly Space Guide

What ARE Sensory Processing Differences?

Humans use our senses to interpret the world. How our brains decode and process, sensory information can significantly impact how we interact with the people we engage with and the environments we enter.

NeuroDivergent people often have sensory processing differences, sometimes referred to as a sensory processing disorder, if our differences cause problems in our ability to live day today in the world.

Every human being, NeuroDivergent or NeuroTypical, has a unique sensory profile that can vary significantly from person to person, even from NeuroDivergent person to NeuroDivergent person.

Evaluating the Spaces You Enter & Creating Spaces that are More Inclusive

While some NeuroDivergent people can be susceptible to environmental sensory stimuli, some NeuroDivergent people may not be sensitive to sensory experiences at all. It can vary significantly from person to person: there is no one-size-fits-all answer. There are, however, things you can do to make spaces more inclusive by design, if you take each of the senses within the human sensory spectrum into consideration.

NOTE from a Sensory Sensitive Human:

As someone with intense sensory issues, whenever I plan to engage with others or venture out into the world, the sensory environment of a space is always one of my first considerations.

I have to weigh the risks, pros, cons and decide what sensory gear I think I will need for the environments I will enter as I'm leaving for the day. As I head out into the world, I'm also planning for the exhaustion, crash, and recovery that will follow time spent in spaces that are often hostile to my senses. I have to think about these things because ignoring them is a risk to my health and safety.

Read through the explanations and suggestions below, then use the yellow box at the end of each sensory breakdown to make your own notes.

Accommodating the 7 Senses

Every human has seven senses, calibrated uniquely to the individual. We may seek out or avoid certain stimuli to balance our sensory systems. We will use my sensory profile below as a starting example.

My Sensory Profile:

Sight/Vision:

Sensory Seeking/Sensory Euphoria: As a kid, I enjoyed turning lights on and off, waving my fingers near my peripherals to watch them on the sides of my view, and staring at spinning fans and pinwheels.

I still find glitter, twinkly lights, and other sparkly or glowing items pleasing and energizing, and I like to unwind by watching visually "soothing" videos, like visual ASMR (Autonomous Sensory Meridian Response).

Sensory Aversions/Troubles: The sun's bright light can be physically painful, and fluorescent lighting makes me physically ill. I can have seizures and migraines from them.

Hearing/Auditory

Sensory Seeking/Sensory Euphoria: Since I was a young person, and still today, music has been one of my main ways to sensory seek and one of my primary sensory euphoria triggers. I cannot put into words the intensely euphoric, physical pleasure or the deep levels of emotion that some songs can bring me.

As a kid (and even now), I would listen to the same song on repeat for hours, taking headphones with me everywhere I went, as a buffer, insulating me from the hostile and unpredictable sounds of the outside world. This sensitivity to music is a tool I've used throughout my life to help combat my sensory sound sensitivities, as the predictable sounds that I have control over can ground me. In contrast, the unpredictable sounds made by the modern world can destabilize and overload me.

Sensory Aversions/Troubles:

I can, and always have been, able to hear and am bothered by sounds that other people often don't even notice. This includes electric sounds that most people can't hear or can easily tune out, like, humming light bulbs, electronic equipment, or a TV that's been left on but with the screen off.

The quiet noises that most people can tune out are not quiet to me and sometimes can drown out the sounds I want to focus on, such as people talking around me.

I can't filter out and isolate the sounds. These audio-processing difficulties can cause me to mishear words and even cause panic, anxiety, and sometimes physical pain, depending on the type, suddenness, and sound volume. Sensory overload from sounds can result in headaches, irritation, and fatigue.

Smell/Olfactory

Sensory Seeking/Sensory Euphoria: I love and always have enjoyed sniffing things that smell good. Most of my euphoric smells are either natural or food smells. As a kid, one of my favorite comfort items at school was my scented markers, pens, and crayons. I still enjoy scented gel pens as an adult.

Sensory Aversions/Troubles:

When I smell something I like, it makes me feel warm and happy, while smelling something unpleasant can cause nausea, panic, elopement, and even vomiting.

Overwhelming smells that frequently cause problems for me include perfumes and cleaners, bodily fluid smells, or any rotten/rancid/dead smell. If I don't run to escape a triggering smell (I may run without thinking if a fragrance is terrible enough), I may experience prolonged sensory overload from the scent.

Taste/Gustatory

Sensory Seeking/Sensory Euphoria:

I LOVE eating bold and flavorful foods, but my tastes were much milder as a child.

As an adult, when people describe food and the ingredients within a dish, I can imagine (with reasonable accuracy) what the dish will taste like. Though I struggle with the executive functioning part of cooking, my sensory system makes me good at imagining dishes and seasoning foods to perfection.

Sensory Aversions/Troubles:

Growing up, I had a very restricted, primarily tan/beige diet consisting of mostly sandwiches, pasta with butter or white sauce, plain burgers, French fries, and chicken nuggets. As an adult, bland foods or foods of the wrong texture are inedible to me, regardless of how hungry I am, and can make me gag.

When I'm overwhelmed or not doing well, my sense of taste will often fail me, and all foods can become tasteless, bland, gross, and unappetizing.

Touch/Tactile

Sensory Seeking/Sensory Euphoria:

I shop for clothes by touch and texture. You can often find me moving through the stores' clothing sections, grasping the shirts' arms, feeling their surfaces, and rubbing the softest ones repeatedly in my hands. If something is soft and fluffy (clothing, toys, animals), my hands will be drawn to it, like moths to a flame.

Sensory Aversions/Troubles:

I get cold VERY easily and can't stand the sensation of moving air on my arms. Certain fabrics and textures of clothing also feel like fire ants biting my skin.

The last two senses are the ones people often forget about, vestibular and proprioception.

Vestibular/Movement

Our vestibular sense helps us orient ourselves and determine where we are in space. When we struggle in this area, we may find it challenging to stay upright in various positions. If this system is dysregulated, we can become dizzy and disoriented. Trouble in this area can also cause people to lose their balance.

This is one sensory area where I am a sensory seeker most of the time, though, during sensory overload, this is often one of the first senses to go.

Sensory Seeking/Sensory Euphoria: I grew up spinning until I was dizzy in the barber chairs of my mother's hair salon. As an adult, I still enjoy spinning and dancing to my favorite songs while on roller skates. Other activities I've always found pleasure in, and still enjoy, include swinging, hanging upside down, and riding slides, rides, and roller coasters.

Sensory Aversions/Troubles: My balance on my two feet isn't the best in general, especially when moving, if I'm not mindful of my steps and movements. In crowded spaces when lots of people around me are moving, it can make me feel if I am also moving.

In addition, when I experience sensory overload, my vestibular system often crashes, causing vertigo, spinning, and vomiting.

Proprioception/Body Awareness

WebMD defines proprioception as "**your body's ability to sense movement, action, and location**. Without proprioception, you wouldn't be able to move without thinking about your next step.[1]" Proprioception also gives us information about how much force to use on objects, such as when opening and closing doors, without slamming or pulling them too hard.

Sensory Seeking/Sensory Euphoria: I was, and still am, someone who needs near-constant sensory input to stay regulated most of the time.

As a kid, I was always in motion (climbing, jumping, swinging, flinging myself onto things), except for when I was squishing my body between the sofa cushions or other pieces of furniture.

As an adult, I still love bear hugs and being squished under heavy people, weighted blankets, and other objects.

Sensory Aversions/Troubles:

I struggle with spatial awareness and motor planning, so not thinking my movements through often leads me to bumping into walls and tables, which also makes driving difficult. I also struggle to know how much pressure I should use when pulling or pushing on objects, which regularly causes me to destroy things I don't intend to break.

I can learn complex movements, such as roller skating and other flow arts, but doing so often takes me longer than it does for people who are more skilled in this area.

---

1. https://www.webmd.com/brain/what-is-proprioception

Those of you who have the privilege of not worrying about sensory overload, I ask you to, please, think carefully about the spaces around you. Think about the areas you work in and the stores and public spaces you enter.

❖ How can you adapt the sensory environments so that people with different sensory profiles can all engage equitably?

❖ What obstacles can you remove or adjust to make **your** spaces more inclusive?

❖ What about accommodating people whose sensory needs are different from one another?

Vision/Sight

People with visual sensitivities may experience painful symptoms from visual overload, such as headaches, migraines, vertigo, nausea, disorientation, and even seizures.

Lighting isn't the only problem for those with visual processing differences. Some people with visual sensitivities may find bold and bright patterns or colors overwhelming, even painful, to look at.

Questions to ask:

Is your space filled with artificial bright lights, strobing or flickering lamps, fixtures, or light glares from external windows with shades that cannot be shut? Are your walls or floors covered in bold patterns and bright colors?

Questions to ask (cont...):

Whenever possible, it is helpful to provide multiple lighting options for your spaces. Create spaces that have bright lighting, as well as less bright spaces. Avoid designing spaces with stripes and other bold patterns or colors, and stick to more neutral pallets and simple designs.

While light glares and bright artificial lighting can be painful and overwhelming for visual sensitivities, some people need bright lights to see appropriately. There are situations in which bright lighting may be required.

Visual Processing Solutions:

❖ Create spaces that have bright lighting, as well as less bright spaces.

❖ Create indoor shade structures, or remove lights above work and other areas for people to create high and low light spaces to moderate their individual needs.

❖ Provide both warm & cool lighting options or custom light options where people can pick the color and tone of lighting that suits their individual needs in that particular moment.

❖ Add dimmer switches to bright lights so that their intensity can be turned down, depending on the needs of the individuals in the room.

❖ Allow the use of sunglasses, shades, and hats, even indoors if needed.

❖ Avoid designing spaces with stripes and other bold patterns or colors, and stick to more neutral pallets and simple designs.

Get Creative!

In spaces that need to have bright lights overhead, depending on ceiling height, you may be able to create indoor shade structures that allow people to move freely between well-lit and more dimly lit spaces.

In meeting rooms, you can often do simple things such as turning the lights in one half of the meeting room down or off and allowing people to sit in whichever lighting suites them best.

If your space does not have enough lighting when the overhead lights have been switched off, you may want to bring in lamps with lower wattages or bulbs with varied color options and dimmers so that the lighting can be changed and customized.

Remember to look at visual processing in your space!

Hearing/Sounds

Just like with visual sensitivity, overload from auditory (hearing) sensitivities can lead to problems such as headaches, migraines, vertigo, and disorientation.

People who experience auditory sensitivities may find sudden or loud noises physically painful and overwhelming. Those who are more sensitive to sounds may be bothered by or unable to tune out sounds that many people can easily ignore, or may not notice.

QUESTIONS TO ASK:

Is everyone in your space expected to work together in one, large, open space? Are there places people can go if they need a quiet moment to think? Are there spaces to complete focused work without the worry of being interrupted?

Are you hosting happy hours, meetings, or educational seminars in busy or loud spaces, such as restaurants, kitchens, or bars? Do your rooms echo? Our air conditioning units, fans, lights, or other pieces of machinery humming?

> **NOTE:** People with an auditory processing disorder may struggle to process words accurately and engage equitably in noisy or busy environments.
>
> These mechanical noises may seem quiet to someone who is not sensory sensitive. Still, those who struggle with auditory overwhelm hear things that others often miss and may find the constant mechanical input draining.

Auditory Processing Solutions:

- ❖ Be mindful of sounds that are created in your space.

- ❖ Address droning and draining sounds that can come from machinery.

- ❖ Avoid placing work, communal, and sensory-friendly areas near humming electric equipment or other commonly loud spaces whenever possible.

❖ Use sound and echo dampening panels in busy or loud spaces—adding fabric surfaces (such as chairs, rugs, drapes, and other furniture can also help absorb sounds).

❖ If you have music playing over a PA system, the easy option would be to stop this and stop forcing everyone to listen to the same music.

❖ Whenever possible, allow, encourage, and provide access to tools that let people have more control over their auditory input, such as personal music with earbuds or noise-canceling headphones, earplugs, or ear defenders.

❖ In office environments, be sure to provide spaces where people who need to work quietly can separate from people working while talking, collaborating, and making more noise.

❖ It may be helpful to utilize small rooms that people can book if they need a moment of solitary quiet. (These small rooms can also be helpful if someone is planning to do a noisy activity and may disturb others, such as a loud phone call.)

Remember to look at auditory processing in your space!

Smell/Scents

People who are more sensitive to smells may need to avoid certain scents.

Like the other senses, smells can overwhelm and cause physical discomfort or sickness, such as nausea or vomiting, may occur with olfactory overload. Scent overloads can cause disorientation, headaches, vertigo, or a person suddenly running away from smells in panic.

Most frequently, smells creep in from kitchens, break rooms, and bathrooms. Bad smells can also come from trash cans and people eating in workspaces. Sometimes fragrances from perfumes and colognes and air fresheners and cleaners can be a significant annoyance for people who are sensitive to smells.

Sniff around your space:

❖ Do you smell anything? Smell is a highly subjective sense. One person's favorite smell maybe someone else's sensory overload or PTSD trigger.

Scent Processing Solutions:

- ❖ Empty any trash cans that contain food at least once a day and make sure trash can lids close and seal, locking in bad smells (especially if the can holds discarded food or human waste products).
- ❖ Ask employees not to wear strong smells such as perfumes and colognes to work.
- ❖ Avoid the use of air fresheners, sprays, candles, and other chemicals. (Choose unscented products whenever possible.)
- ❖ Ensure **high smell areas** (bathrooms, breakrooms, kitchens) have doors that close and good ventilation.
- ❖ Keep work areas, common areas, education, and meeting spaces away from **high smell areas** whenever possible.

Remember to look at smell/scents in your space!

Tactile/Touch

Tactile sensitivities can mean people may be sensitive to certain fabrics and clothing. Some people, who are touch-sensitive, may dislike (or possibly feel pain) when others touch them.

Tactile Processing Solutions

❖ Don't touch people without their consent, especially if they are not looking at you or expecting to be touched.

❖ When planning activities, consider that some physical touch from others may be unwelcome and unpleasant. If leading activities that may include physical touch, be sure to provide options that do not require physical contact.

❖ If your organization has a dress code, consider ways to allow for more flexibility to allow those with tactile sensitivity to avoid fabrics and clothing that can feel suffocation, itchy, or painful.

❖ Be mindful of the fabrics you use to furnish your spaces. Use soft and inviting materials, avoiding anything itchy or harsh.

Remember to look at tactile/touch processing in your space!

Taste & Food

People with taste (or texture) sensitivities may have a limited food pallet.

Some of us may be taste seekers. Those who are hypersensitive (less/underly sensitive) to taste may crave and seek out bold foods and flavors, struggling to eat bland foods.

Other people with sensory processing differences may be taste-avoiders if they are hypersensitive (more sensitive) to how taste is processed in the brain. Taste avoiders may only eat very bland foods, avoiding heavily seasoned or spicy foods.

NeuroDivergent people are also more likely to experience co-occurrence of food sensitivities and food allergies. Because of this, many of us will stick to foods that we know are "safe foods" that won't cause overwhelming or digestive distress.

Taste Processing Solutions

❖ When food is involved, it can be beneficial to provide the menu to all guests in advance, allowing for multiple meal choices to accommodate people with varied pallets.

❖ Always ask about dietary restrictions and food allergies, and accommodate those dietary needs.

❖ If possible, allow people to bring their own food and snacks to your space.

Remember to look at taste in your space!

Proprioception & Vestibular

Proprioception is the ability to feel where your body/limbs are in space, and **Vestibular** is the sense that controls movement and balance.

While sensory seekers in these two senses may appear to be always in motion, people who are hypersensitive to these senses can be prone to motion sickness.

People who struggle with proprioception may be clumsy or experience difficulty with fine motor control.

Proprioception & Vestibular Processing Solutions

❖ When planning events or managing people, incorporate and encourage movement breaks, especially if people sit for extended periods.

❖ Provide ways for sensory seekers to get the movement they need. Are there places people can go for walks, run, exercise, jump, climb, and engage the senses of balance and movement?

❖ Offer alternative seating options such as rocking or wobble chairs, beanbags, ball chairs, floor chairs, standing and exercise desks.

❖ Provide sensory items such as fidget and stim tools.

Remember to look at Proprioception &
Vestibular processing in your space!

Sensory Rooms & Sensory Spaces

Even in ideal situations and environments, those of us who experience sensory differences may need to remove ourselves from overstimulating environments from time to time to recharge ourselves and prevent overload.

The need to recuperate means that it is crucial for public, work, and educational spaces to have designated areas where people can take a break and recharge as necessary, without fear of how it may be perceived.

Creating Sensory Friendly Spaces

Sensory spaces should be free of bright lighting or light glares, quiet, and should include comfortable sensory-friendly seating options.

Include sensory aides, such as stim and fidget tools, headphones, and soothing music. Art supplies, crayons, markers, and drawing paper can also be great ways to ground oneself.

You can create sensory areas that groups can use and private sensory rooms or spaces if people need to retreat away from others fully. Ideally, both options would be available whenever possible.

Remember to look at your sensory space!

Meeting Each Person & Their Individual Human Needs

Although we can try to make our spaces as inclusive as possible, every single human being has a unique sensory profile that can vary significantly from person to person. One person's idea of sensory bliss and perfection may be the next person's sensory nightmare.

You Should Ask These Questions:

There is no one size fits all answer. **That's why you have to ASK:**

- ❖ Are you comfortable? If not, is there anything I can do or provide to increase your comfort level?

- ❖ Is there anything you need or is there anything that I can do for you?

- ❖ Is this lighting okay?

- ❖ Can I turn the lights up or down for you?

- ❖ Is it too loud or busy here for you?

- ❖ Are you able to concentrate with the current amount of background noise?

- ❖ Is the temperature okay for you?

- ❖ Would you like to move someplace calmer?

Remember to think more about making a sensory-friendly space!

NeuroDivergent Pace

NeuroDivergent workers may have variable energy reserves, and may need to adjust their schedules accordingly.

NeuroDivergent Pace vs **NeuroTypical Pace**

It is important to remember that NeuroDivergent pace is often variable from NeuroTypical pace. Some of us will peak and wane at varied times of the day, or may have periods of increased productivity, followed by crashes.

Some NeuroDivergent people may hyperfocus or get "in the zone", working on something without stopping for 12 hours straight (or more), while other NeuroDivergent people may need to space out their work, taking many breaks between tasks.

Neither style of work is wrong, and both can create quality results.

The employee who was on a roll, and couldn't stop until they felt they were at an appropriate stopping point, may be worn down after binge working 12 or more hours nonstop, and may need recovery time between projects.

The employee who gets all their work done by the deadline, but must take lots of breaks between tasks may be your most dedicated and reliable employee, if you empower them to work in the ways that suit them best.

Differences in NeuroDivergent Pace in Action

Before I knew I was NeuroDivergent, I was chronically burnt out, or teetering just on the edge of burnout, because I was treating my NeuroDivergent brain like a NeuroTypical one.

I didn't know I was NeuroDivergent for the first part of my life because NeuroDiversity is an invisible diversity that can be easily overlooked by the untrained eye. If I didn't want you to know I was NeuroDivergent, you would never know.

Not knowing this important fact about myself had a huge impact on me.

I was not in a good place when I found out I was Autistic; however, the knowledge I've gained has changed my life, helping me to get myself back on track.

Since discovering my NeuroDivergence, over six years ago now, I have learned something I wish I could have known all along:

> *That I can only be truly happy and successful if I am able to be my authentic self, permitted to exist and comfortable in my own skin*—as I'm sure is the case for each person, whatever their Neurotype, who reads this book.

WE NEED TO BE ACCEPTED AS WE ARE!

People need to be accepted as their whole person—both strengths and weaknesses.

Hiding parts of who I am was preventing me from moving forward in life, and getting help when I needed it. In my thirties, I had to teach myself to ask for help, because I had learned to mask those weaknesses, instead of speaking up for my needs, because I had been hiding them for so long.

NeuroDivergent Camouflaging (Masking) & Burnout

NeuroDivergent Masking is when a NeuroDivergent person consciously or subconsciously hides or masks their Divergent traits, in order to blend in or appear NeuroTypical. It is important to note that this camouflaging is done in self-defense. It is not intended to be manipulative or deceptive.

NeuroDivergent Masking in Action

Over the years, I've learned to compensate for (or mask) my struggles and differences, but not all NeuroDivergent people can hide how they are different.

For those of us who do mask, this ability to camouflage may fluctuate throughout a person's lifetime.

When I'm not doing well my ability to mask/hide my struggles is diminished, and my areas of weakness become more pronounced.

I may regress, as it's sometimes called in children—or BURN OUT—and my ability to "function" as expected (when compared to my NeuroTypical peers) may be decreased.

Camouflaging is hard on NeuroDivergent people for many reasons, on top of the obvious problems having to hide your authentic self would cause for anyone.

Camouflaging in NeuroDivergent people has been tied to poor mental health impacts, such as increased anxiety and depression—which is alarming, considering that many NeuroDivergent people also have diagnosable co-occurring mental health conditions, and that suicide rates are high amongst NeuroDivergent populations.

NeuroDivergent Burnout

Some NeuroDivergent people have a "talent" for pushing themselves past where they should push themselves. Many NeuroDivergent people have and will repeatedly experience NeuroDivergent Burnout in their lives.

> **Autistic Burnout** "is defined as the intense physical, mental or emotional exhaustion, often accompanied by a loss of skills, that some Autistic people experience. Many Autistic people say it results mainly from the cumulative effect of having to navigate a world that is designed for neurotypical people."

While Autistic Burnout is the most common form of burnout discussed and studied, similar burnouts can occur across all NeuroTypes.

If you've ever heard of regression (loss of skills) in NeuroDivergent children: this is the same thing. MANY of us are burnt out as CHILDREN, long before we reach adulthood with its extra stressors.

These burnouts tend to be caused by stressors in an NeuroDivergent person's environment, often including sensory distress and other sensory related triggers. Change, good or bad, can be another burnout trigger for many NeuroDivergent people.

NeuroDivergent camouflaging and burnout are often related, as masking can, and frequently does lead NeuroDivergent people to burning out. THEN when NeuroDivergent People do burn out, it can become harder for us to camouflage.

When this happens NeuroTypical people often won't react well, expecting the NeuroDivergent Person to keep the mask up, even when they have become too exhausted by life to do so.

I've hit the burnout phase multiple times in life, the first time being when I was eleven years old. Then again in my teens, and again in the workplace, leading to my late Autistic discovery at the age of twenty-nine.

Story of a Burned Out AuDHDer

I got stuck an endless cycle of burning myself out, because I didn't understand that my pace could and should be different from the pace of people around me. I didn't understand my differences, or how to speak up and advocate for myself.

Now that I know I'm NeuroDivergent I have been learning what I need, how my mind works, and ways to work with my mind instead of against it.

One of the best things I've ever done was modify my work schedule, moving from the more traditional model to one that optimizes when my brain is feeling most efficient.

If left to manage myself, **I can often complete tasks I am well suited for more quickly**, and often with more accuracy than most NeuroTypicals I know, DEPENDING ON THE TASK. **Tasks I'm poorly suited for, can also take me longer**, cannot be completed as well. This is one reason why it is important to ensure a good skills match when assigning tasks.

I also work around my brain, and block off work in chunks that make sense for me. In the mornings, because communication is more work for me than it is for Allistic (non-Autistic) people, I'm often not ready for talking to other humans until later in the day, when I'm fully awake.

Other people can be exhausting, and will often drain the creativity right out of me, so I plan my days accordingly. It has been helpful for me to tackle quiet, focused, work that requires creativity and inspiration in the morning, when I'm fresh.

Flexible Schedules & Start Times

Different people will find their energy peaks at different times of day. Some people may work best in the mornings, but other people may do better starting later in the day, or even late at night.

Flexible start times and schedules are wonderful, if people's positions allow for them.

For example:

With a flexible start time, you can allow people to start their day between 7 & 10 am, shifting their day back and working later or getting off earlier in the day as appropriate.

With full flexible scheduling, you can allow people to work as they have energy, and work their schedule around their peaks and lows, as long as they are able to get their work done.

These types of schedules are great for people with disabilities and NeuroDivergent traits, but also benefit everyone, because it promotes a sense of trust and autonomy. Plus, NeuroTypical people also have their own peaks and troughs.

Real life example:

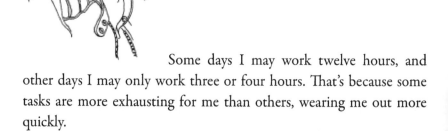

Some days I may work twelve hours, and other days I may only work three or four hours. That's because some tasks are more exhausting for me than others, wearing me out more quickly.

In one organization I worked for, we all had fully remote work with fully flexible scheduling (except for specific occasions).

In this organization, parents in the company benefited from being able to work around their children's home school schedules—when schools closed during COVID, for example.

Everyone was responsible for making sure the team was aware when they were going to be unavailable.

Each person was responsible for updating their own Google Calendar, and everyone on the team had access to see everyone else's schedules.

We would remind each other of our upcoming schedule if there were any special notes about the upcoming week in our weekly team meetings, or to remind the team closer to any scheduled time off, as appropriate.

People were also encouraged to check people's calendars before reaching out to them, as some of us would also put things like "quiet work time please do not disturb" on our calendars, to ensure we got the focus time we needed.

The trouble with hourly work for some NeuroDivergent employees

Hours based work can be a bit of a slap in the face for those who complete work more quickly than everyone else, because it means the fastest people do most of, and often an unfair amount of, the work, compared to everyone else.

In hours-based pay systems, top performers—those who work faster and harder—are more likely to keep pushing themselves until they eventually burn out and leave.

Real life example

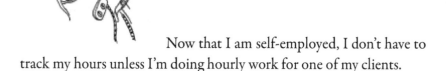

Now that I am self-employed, I don't have to track my hours unless I'm doing hourly work for one of my clients.

Even though I'm not trying to cram in hours, like I once did, I often still will work more than I intend to, especially when I enjoy or am passionate about the work. I focus more on the actual tasks and deadlines I have over the number of hours of work that I need to cram in.

Though I don't clock in or count time, I DO keep a very accurate calendar, adjusting it with all my tasks, calls, breaks, and deadlines, helping me plan the work that needs to be done, in the best way I'm able to do it. I'm still able to track my hours and tasks in this way, and it means I'm fitting my schedule to my own needs, rather than trying to cram it into someone's else's.

Of course, working on my own makes it is much easier for me to customize the rules to my organization to fit my particular needs. When working with larger teams, you must consider how your policies and procedures impact everyone on the team, and what you can do to better accommodate their different needs.

Policies & Procedures for the Benefit of All Employees

We already spoke about "" in the previous sections about "" and "". This is just one benefit that many people with disabilities, both visible and invisible, may need that, when offered globally, instead of being guarded heavily by a gatekeeper, can benefit everyone within an organization.

Don't Create Separate Pipelines, Dependent on Disclosures and Diagnosis

When we gatekeep accessibility, instead of building it into our organizational design, we force people with disabilities to out themselves, whether they feel ready to do so or not.

This can separate us from our peers, pushing us into separate pipelines, where the people in the main pipeline are left gazing upon us with envious eyes.

This separation can create a hostile work environment for people with disabilities, because the things we need are often things everybody wants and can benefit from.

"Why do THEY get special treatment?"—is a common complaint from peers and other organizational members who would also like the accommodations (or even just the knowledge that they are available to them) that are sometimes reserved ONLY for employees with a documented medical need. It also unfairly affects those who do need accommodations, but fear outing their NeuroDivergence due to negative experiences in their past.

Accommodating NeuroDivergent employees is leveling the playing field, creating equity across the board, so they can access systems that weren't designed with their needs taken into consideration. It's not special treatment, but when everyone is suffering together in a broken system, it can feel that way to people who aren't getting the help they need.

NeuroDivergent people are the modern workplace version of canaries in the coal mines. We can be more sensitive to our environments, and may even become physically and/or mentally unwell in a toxic setting, before NeuroTypical people do.

Built in accessibility is accessibility for everyone. We need you to make these changes, and it is likely that many of your NeuroTypical team members will also appreciate the benefits of having a more accessible workplace.

Creating Environments Where ALL Human Minds Can THRIVE

A Global Pandemic and the New Era of Employment

It's not that "people don't want to work anymore", it's that people are starting to realize how limited and precious our time here on earth is.

Since 2020, we have been living in a world of chaos, death, crisis, fear, and destruction. Many of us have lost people we loved, jobs we thought were stable, and had our hopes, dreams, and plans ripped away.

Suddenly all around the world people were forced to slow down or speed up, as our lives were uprooted, displaced, and, in some cases, destroyed, by the recent pandemic.

The global crisis has forced many of us to look more closely at, and have some serious discussions about, how mental health is essential to other parts of our health, as well as the impact that workplaces can have on our minds.

Employees are asking employers for more accountability, and organizations that struggle to shift away from their exploitative practices, are also struggling to find staff who are willing to be exploited.

Now more than ever, people are beginning to understand the importance and necessity of taking time away from work, for our physical and emotional well-being.

Through the promotion of happier, healthier, more human friendly workplaces, you can become a more desirable place to work, reduce burnout, prevent employee turnover, and increase retention.

Burnout and Overwork is an Organizational Problem

Burnout isn't good for ANY employee, regardless of NeuroType.

As discussed in previous sections of this book, employee burnout is bad for organization, because the people in the organization who burn out often tend to be the higher performers, who care the most about their jobs and work.

It is that very dedication and drive that will burn an organization's top performers out. Many organizational structures put the people who care the most through the wringer, squeezing them until there's nothing left, they stop caring, and then leave.

Employee burnout isn't an employee problem, it's an employer problem.

For many years we have failed to recognize this, blaming employees for failing when being put through abusive organizational systems.

Treating Humans like HUMANS

NeuroDivergent people cannot thrive in workplaces that treat them like machines and not people. Even NeuroTypical people, who may fare better for longer, will eventually become miserable, and therefore less productive, in exploitative environments.

People are not machines. We are susceptible to burnouts and breakdowns if we don't rest at the right moments. Pushing ourselves to always be productive, even on our worst days, is cruel, and is disrespectful of our human dignity.

Employers (should) want people to come to work as their best self: happy, productive, rested, and empowered. Forcing people to work when their minds are elsewhere, or in need of rest, isn't good business, as this inevitably will produce half-assed, subpar work, done with less quality, care, and attention than an employee could do on a day when they feel closer to being their best.

Too many workplaces have lost their humanity. Those organizations must evolve, or their distance from the human aspect of HR (their human resources), will eventually lead to their downfall.

People are waking up to the exploitative nature that many companies have adopted, and are becoming less and less likely to subject themselves to these exploitative organizations and systems.

It's time to start treating your employees like people. The NeuroDivergent people on your team, and your overall organizational health, depends on it.

Paid Time Off (PTO)

It's the Law

Though it may vary in your country, the Americans with Disabilities Act (ADA) states that employers need to provide reasonable accommodations to employees with disabilities, including invisible disabilities and differences such as NeuroDivergence.

According to the Equal Employment Opportunity Commission (EEOC), the agency that enforces the ADA in America, "a leave" or taking time off of work can be a reasonable accommodation."

Leave can be taken all at once, or spread out as needed. The amount of time may vary depending on multiple factors, including your local laws, but generally, leave under the ADA will be capped at two weeks, with some exceptions.

> *Is your organization ahead of the curve, offering paid sick, personal, and vacation days that any team member can use if needed? OR are you just doing the bare minimum?*

Paid Personal Time Off

Another example of something that NeuroDivergent people and their supporters and caregivers need is access to appropriate PTO (Personal, and Sick Time policies that include mental health days, and time to care for family members and loved ones if needed).

Do you offer personal PTO that can be utilized if an employee is needing a day off at the last minute, or do you only offer scheduled paid time off to your employees?

Personal paid time off is typically a supplement to your organization's vacation and paid sick time policies. This type of short-term leave can be planned or unplanned, and can typically be used for any reason.

Can people take the time they need without being penalized for having human needs? Are you taking these needs into consideration when you build your organization? Are you treating your people like people?

What types of PTO are there? More in the following sections.

Paid Vacation Time

Paid vacation is a commonly offered benefit that employers will offer their employees. Vacation time is intended for scheduled rest and relaxation time as a break from work, or for scheduled, pre-planned, personal matters.

Employers, typically, ask that vacation time be scheduled in advance.

But, do you release bookable PTO in chunks and have everyone scramble to book what they want/need, causing stress and unhappiness, especially in those who move more slowly or need time to think and check dates? Or do you have a system that more fairly allows all employees the time they need to request PTO?

Some, more flexible employers, may also allow employees to use vacation time for unexpected absences.

Paid Sick Time

More and more cities and states in America[1] are beginning to require employers to offer paid sick leave to their employees, so that people don't feel pressured to work when sick (perhaps even more so now, due to what we've all experienced with COVID-19 recently).

Unlike vacation time, which is typically planned in advance, paid sick time is intended for unexpected absences that are hard to plan for, such as in the case of sickness or physical injury of an employee or their family member or other relative (such as a spouse, child, domestic partner, or parent).

Extended Leave (STD Insurance & FMLA)

What about extended personal or medical leave, if someone has a health emergency or needs to take time for a child or loved one?

Do you have a standard procedure in place in case someone on your team needs extra time away from work?

What about STD (short-term disability) insurance?

Is anyone in your organization familiar with FMLA (Family and Medical Leave Act) laws, and able to guide employees through that process if needed?

Do you have paid leave for new parents that does not discriminate based on the gender of the parent? If you have family leave, is it broader and does it allow for someone to care for an older member or parent?

Combined PTO Bank

Many employers are now offering employees a combined PTO bank that employees can use for any reason, and includes vacation, personal, sick time, and any other reason an employee may request time off. This

---

1. https://www.shrm.org/resourcesandtools/legal-and-compliance/employment-law/pages/state-local-paid-sick-leave-chart.aspx

leave can be planned or unplanned, allowing employees more flexibility in the use of time off.

Combined PTO banks can also be less invasive for employees with disabilities, as they don't require constant explanations, or the sharing of private medical information, when asking for time off. As long as the employee has time available, they are able to request their time off as needed.

Unlimited PTO Policy

Some employers are ditching PTO banks all together, and offering their teams unlimited PTO.

Unlimited PTO in Action

Working on my own, I embrace unlimited PTO and take time off as needed (as long as I am getting through the work that I need to do, in a reasonable amount of time). Doing so has helped me to have a major mind shift, which has been wonderful for my NeuroDivergent mind, since I stopped counting and tracking my PTO days, and also stopped counting each hour I work.

In the past, when I worked in hourly spaces it was easy to focus on how many hours I was working, rather than how well I was working, which was actually a distraction from the work I was hired to do.

With hourly work, employees are thinking about the hours they owe and are cramming in. This means they may be more focused on the clock and time than on the quality and efficiency of their work.

Organizations with unlimited PTO that don't pay hourly wages have a very different culture than teams who live and die by the clock.

Those of us who have made this shift are more focused on the effectiveness, efficiency, and quality of our work. We drive for results, and the clock isn't an obstacle to our work or personal lives. In fact, a lot of time and mental energy is freed up when we no longer have to think about cramming in the right number of hours on the clock.

These systems can also be less work for your managers, and the HR team too, as there is now less PTO to track and approve.

Hourly systems can unintentionally punish employees who work efficiently, or burn them out.

Because your top performers may be able to do as much work as two or more unseasoned team members in a day, they are likely pulling more weight than the people around them. Eventually, this can bring their morale down.

Why would an employee, who can work three times as fast as their peers, push to do more work than everyone else?

Because they genuinely care, and they are dedicated. This dedication is what makes your top performers more vulnerable to burnout.

NOTE about Unlimited PTO & Passionate Team Members: When switching to an unlimited PTO system, your most dedicated employees may feel uncomfortable taking advantage of unlimited PTO policies, or even using PTO in general.

Some organizations with unlimited PTO, including one I worked in previously, can develop a culture where employees with unlimited PTO take less time off, because they feel guilty for using the benefits they are entitled to.

The people who care the most about the company are less likely to take time off, while the people who care less about the organization may take more time off, abusing the policy.

One solution that can help to prevent the burnout of your top performers is having a Minimum PTO Policy, regardless if your PTO is unlimited or not.

It is also still a good idea to track when people are out on leave, in the event someone does abuse an unlimited PTO policy.

How do I know if someone is abusing an unlimited PTO policy? As long as employees are completing all assigned tasks by the deadline, in task-based work, they can take PTO as wanted. If performance slips and deadlines are missed, or work becomes sloppy and rushed, while employees are taking lots of PTO, this may constitute abuse.

Remember, when looking into potential abuse of an unlimited PTO policy, it is important to consider if someone is taking time off for vacation or if they are out for an injury, emergency, or illness.

Questions to Ask:

❖ Is a PTO bank or unlimited PTO something your organization can, or already is offering?

❖ If not, what obstacles are currently preventing you from making this change (assuming you want to—and you really should)?

Minimum PTO Policy

If your organization has a paid time off policy or an unlimited paid time off policy, you may want to consider also implementing a minimum PTO policy that requires employees to take a minimum number of paid days (PTO) off from work each year.

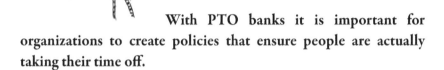

With PTO banks it is important for organizations to create policies that ensure people are actually taking their time off.

I've worked in organizations with both PTO banks and unlimited PTO, so short-staffed departments felt as if they could not take time off, and were often working more and taking less PTO than if they would have with set PTO or forced PTO.

It is important to make sure people are able to take their time off.

If your organization chooses to offer your employees the benefit of PTO, employees should be given the opportunity—and encouraged—to take advantage of it, and not made to feel guilty for taking advantage of the benefits they are entitled to, per your own organizational policy.

Set clear expectations in advance, otherwise your hardest and most dedicated workers will face increased risk of burnout, productivity problems, and eventually, turnover.

Flextime, Compressed, and Four Day Work Weeks

All over the world, workers are beginning to place more value on having a better work life balance. Because of this recent shift, employers that offer flexible work options may be in higher demand than those who offer traditional work schedules.

Flexible schedules, flexible work, or flex time is a schedule that allows employees to shift and customize their arrival and departure times. With flexible schedules employees are empowered to choose a schedule that works best with their individual lifestyle and needs. This flexibility can be extremely beneficial for both people with disabilities, working parents, and any human who has a life or wants to have a life outside of work.

In organizations that implement flexible schedules, employees typically will still work the same amount of hours they would within a traditional work schedule, merely adjusted to their needs.

There are multiple ways an employer can implement flexible scheduling, and choosing the best option(s) for your organization can make a big difference in your office.

The flexibility that these types of scheduling arrangements give, also may improve employee morale.

NeuroDivergent people who struggle with time blindness, or executive functioning issues (something particularly common in ADHDers), may benefit from not having to arrive at an "exact time", reducing tardiness, and the need for HR people to track late arrivals, as people who show up late will also stay late, or make up the time later in the week.

Flexible work arrangements also may increase an organization's ability to attract and retain more diverse employees and teams, because these types of schedules can be better for people with disabilities, and workers who have children, parents, or loved ones to care for.

It's good for EVERYONE!

People have less need to take time off for personal business, because they are able to shift their schedules around to accommodate for appointments without disrupting day-to-day business operations.

In addition to making a position more desirable for potential candidates, flextime also may improve employee satisfaction, engagement, and retention, due to the increased amount of respect and autonomy employees with these schedules often experience. This can prevent turnover by increasing employee attendance and helping to create happier, more productive, and engaged, employees.

Flex time during core business hours

Depending on your individual organization or team goals and needs, you may decide to require members of your team to be present during core business hours.

For example, you could require all employees or members of a team to be in the office between 10am and 2pm, with flexibility to come in earlier, or leave earlier in the day, as long as they are present during the core business hours.

The core time, when all employees are required to be online or at your work site, may vary, depending upon the job requirements and operational needs of each team, and the organization more broadly.

NOTE: It may be advisable to ask people to stagger lunches with other team members, if you have phones, front desk, or customer service needs that cannot be put on hold without interrupting business.

Flex time outside of core business hours

Some flexible schedules allow members of a team to work at any time, from anywhere in the world, as long as they are able to keep up with and meet organizational needs.

You also may want to implement a policy that requires employees to work a specific minimum and/or maximum number of hours per pay period.

NOTE: Flexible scheduling may not be appropriate for all organizations, roles, or employees. Unfortunately, there are environments and jobs that make this type of schedule impossible.

Variable Schedules

Variable schedules are very flexible, and can vary week-to-week and day-to-day.

Employees who have variable schedules may come in at different times on different days of the week, or work more hours one day, then work a shorter day another day.

Variable schedules don't require team members to set their hours, and can be beneficial when applied correctly.

Because these types of schedules don't require a set number of hours, extra communication is necessary, to ensure all job duties are covered and managers know when team members are available or not.

Compressed Work Weeks

Another scheduling option that has increased in popularity in recent years is the compressed work week.

With this alternative scheduling method, employees still work the standard 40 hours a week, but they do so over a shorter period of time. Instead of doing 40 hours—8 per day in a five-day work week—some employers may choose to offer, or implement across the board, a four-day work week consisting of four 10-hour days.

Employers get the same number of working hours, but employees have longer weekends and more days off.

Four-day work weeks (32 hours or less)

Four-day work weeks are different from compressed work weeks, because they allow employees more time off by reducing their required work hours to 32 or less per work week. Typically, with these schedules employees will work between 28 & 32 hours a week over four days, and have 3 days off a week.

If the idea of allowing employees to work less hours a week for the same pay scares you, and you're still unsure if reducing hours could work in your workplace, consider that tired overworked employees are nowhere near as productive as well rested employees. If you're unsure, you could begin with a trial of one or two departments, or specific high-performing workers, ensuring that everyone understands that this is a viability test, which will then be considered for further use.

Organizations that embrace shorter, four-day work weeks, report happier employees, who show more dedication to the work they do. Sick days and unplanned absences may also be decreased, due to reduced workplace stress, and employees having enough time off to stay fresh and rested.

Customized Schedules

As people start to value their time more, allowing workers to set their own schedules (within reason) will likely be a benefit that continues to increase in demand and value, making your organization more attractive to potential new talent.

From a NeuroDiversity and disability perspective, these types of schedules can be extremely beneficial for people with differing needs.

Some people are more productive earlier in the day, running out of steam early. There are also people who take a long time to get going, and are fresher at night.

Instead of asking people to work when they aren't the best version of themselves, you can offer employees the chance to customize their schedules. This allows employees to have better balance between life and work, and also can be beneficial, due to people being more efficient when they are working.

You can even offer a mixture of these above types of work week, allowing your employees to pick and use the one that most suits them (and allowing them, with reasonable notification, to switch, if their needs change).

Customized and Flexible Schedules in Action

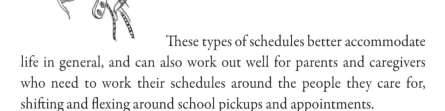

These types of schedules better accommodate life in general, and can also work out well for parents and caregivers who need to work their schedules around the people they care for, shifting and flexing around school pickups and appointments.

In the most recent organization I worked for which utilized customized schedules, when parents suddenly became teachers during remote schooling at the start of the pandemic, our team members with kids at home were able to work their schedules around their kids' school needs, and were still able to participate in and complete their job duties.

Because we were a People First company, we prioritized the human needs of our people, bringing the human back to human resources, and the "L word" (love) back into the workplace (as my former boss would have said).

When work life balance is properly supported, and made a priority by organizational leaders, the side effects may include (but are not limited to) increased productivity and improved morale across the organization.

It's About Trust—Don't Let Fear Lead You

Pushback against flexible and customized schedules is often rooted in fear that employees within the organization cannot be trusted to do their work if they are unsupervised. Some employers worry their employees will sit on their sofas watching Netflix all day, or cut out early to go fishing.

If these fears are all too familiar to you, you could have a much bigger problem within your organization: TRUST ISSUES.

Do you trust your employees, and do your employees trust their leadership? If the answer is "no" in any direction, it can cause huge problems for the health of your organization.

 Trust is crucial, and there are a lot of questions you should ask yourself if you uncover a possible problem of busted trust within your organization.

❖ Are you hiring the wrong people?

❖ Is it bad leadership?

❖ Are your policies and procedures disrupting trust?

❖ Are you burning your workers out?

There is more about trust in the "" section of this book. You can skip back now to read about why you need "", to support NeuroDivergent people, if I've piqued your interest here.

Promoting Flexibility for Shift & Front-line Workers

Depending on the department, role or task, some employees may need to be available in order to ensure continued business operations, such as people working retail, customer service, and other shift work.

Though still very possible, providing flexible scheduling options to these employees may require more creativity and attention.

Shift work

With more and more businesses offering goods and services 24 hours a day, there is an increased need for people to be available to work around the clock.

Most people are familiar with shift work. Customer facing establishments, such as retail stores, tech support lines, and restaurants typically operate using shift workers.

Shift work is typically done in rotations, one team arriving, and then passing the baton to the next team, and then the team after, allowing the company to operate for a full 24 hours every day.

Though there may be benefits for the organization, and some employees may even prefer shift work, there is some evidence that working at inconsistent times may be bad for your mental and physical health, leading to disrupted and disordered sleeping habits.

Because exhausted employees are not able to show up to work as their best selves, they may be less productive. Depending on the job, tired employees can also be a dangerous liability.

Managers should be consistent when scheduling shift workers, offering them regular slots to lessen the risk of disordered sleeping and burnout for these team members. This is especially important for workers who keep your business running through the night and early morning. Ensure you know what your employees need, and schedule accordingly when possible.

Part-time schedules

Part-time jobs are a traditional flexible scheduling option that can work well for shift workers. In the United States part time is typically considered anyone who works less than 35 hours per week, though some employers may define full and part time differently.

Some people may think part time jobs are just for the service industry, however offering part-time positions in vast professional settings can help an organization to retain more of its talented professionals.

There are some NeuroDivergent people, and people with other disabilities who cannot regularly handle working a full forty hour work week.

Offering part time schedules to employees who want to work, but are unable to or do not want to work full time can be attractive to those employees, as well as parents, students, older people, and other people with disabilities.

Split Shifts

Split shifts are another way employers can create flexibility for employees. With split shifts, you work half way through your shift, then take a long, extended break, before returning to finish your shift several hours later.

This type of shift may be beneficial for people who find their workplace's sensory environment to be busy or overwhelming, and need time to step away and decompress, in order to get through the entire work day.

These scheduling arrangements can also help people who need to handle appointments or family obligations during the day.

Job-sharing

Another option when a position needs more coverage than a part time role will allow, is to offer job-sharing. With job-sharing, two part time employees split the tasks, accountability for, and coverage of one full-time position.

Often tasks will be divided up according to availability and individual aptitude and skill.

Job sharing only works if both people in one role are well suited to one another. If two employees sharing one role are not compatible with one another, this type of schedule is likely to cause more harm than good, as people sharing roles have to be exceptionally good at teamwork, individual accountability, and communication (between each other and leadership).

Remote Working/Telecommuting

Working from home or remote work, sometimes called "telecommuting", is where employees are allowed to work from home, coffee shops, planes, trains, and even beaches (if the Wi-Fi and cell signal are good enough).

If properly implemented, with a healthy organizational culture, the benefits of offering remote working may include lower costs for office space and other office related expenses, an increased talent pool, and better productivity overall.

Remote Work Success Story

When I was first diagnosed Autistic, at the age of 29, one of the first major realizations I had was that I am someone who, if expected to do work that requires focus and thought, can work more effectively and efficiently alone at home, where I have control over the environment and can manage my own pace and can limit distractions.

I am also someone who needs control over my sensory environment, in order to prevent painful sensory overloads, migraines, and other neurological health problems.

Limited exposure to my sensory triggers, such as fluorescent lighting may only cause minor discomfort, however, continued exposure for multiple hours a week (as is often required for office jobs) can cause me to experience serious health complications.

Allowing me to work from home means I am able to work for more hours and do better quality work.

If I am also able to set my own pace, I have less risk of burning out.

Knowing my employer supports me and cares about what I need to be happy and healthy, means I am more likely to be loyal to my employer, and less likely to leave or seek out other employment opportunities.

This isn't just true for me. Most employees do better work when they are feeling supported, trusted, and appreciated.

Many People Work More Effectively at Home

For a long time, employers feared loss of control and less supervision would lead to lazy employees, sleeping on sofas and playing video games all day.

These fears meant many organizations and leaders resisted allowing employees to access remote work options. Then something happened...

In the spring of 2020, when countries, states, and cities, all over the world went into lockdown, many businesses who could not operate remotely, were forced to close their doors for weeks, months, and some permanently.

Many who were successful were people in industries who were deemed essential, and those who were brave enough (or forced) to embrace remote work.

As a person with multiple disabilities that remote work can make easier, I have been working remotely for years, even before the pandemic. It is an accommodation that I've almost had to beg for in years past, that has now become standard for many organizations, almost overnight.

Not every role or task can be done remotely.

You may need employees to come into the office from time to time to work on projects or for meetings. There are also different types of remote work, and varied flexibility that can be given, depending on your organization's unique needs.

Full time remote work

Full time remote work is when an employee is fully remote and not expected to come to the office for meetings and projects, except in very special circumstances (that are typically pre-agreed upon when the employee is hired or moved to remote work).

Part time remote work

Part time remote work is when an employee works part time at an employer's physical location and part time from home or another location of the employees choosing.

With part time remote work, an employer may require team members to be at the office a minimum number of days a week, or on specific days of the week, allowing the employee to work remotely the rest of the time.

As-needed remote work

As-needed remote work is the most restrictive form of remote work.

Though most people would appreciate more flexibility, there will always be roles and responsibilities that don't allow for people to regularly be away. In those roles, employees may be allowed to work remotely in specific situations, with approval from their supervisor.

As the name suggests, as-needed remote work is offered temporarily, on a short-term situational case-by-case basis, and only offered as needed.

Legal Compliance

Every state and country in the world have different rules and regulations regarding schedules, wage, and remote work. This book was written in the United States (in Texas), so be aware that the laws may be very different in your part of the world.

It is the employer's job to know, understand, and abide by the local and global laws that impact your organization and team. If you employ people remotely in multiple states and countries, this means also knowing the laws of the states and countries that your employees work in.

Open Offices

Intended to be collaborative and fun, open offices are a popular option for creative agencies and tech spaces, but these work pits can be overwhelming for those employees who may prefer a calm quiet workspace, such as someone with a sensory processing difference, or a difficulty focusing with business or background noise.

Collaboration is wonderful, and these collaborative spaces can add benefits, but even the most extroverted, sensory seeking humans, who thrive in busy and chaotic environments, may situationally need time to work in a more quiet, focused environment (especially if up against a deadline, learning new skills, or completing tasks that fall outside of their current comfort or skill level).

Focused work time is important, and necessary for people to create quality work.

❖ If your workspace utilizes an open office design, try to create spaces for employees to work away from typical office noise and commotion.

❖ You should also consider providing or allowing the use of noise-canceling headphones while working in open office areas.

Hot-Desking

Hot-Desking is a tactic that "forces your employees to stay flexible" by keeping them off-guard, always wondering where they are going to sit next.

This tactic may not work well, and can even be stressful for employees who prefer (and may even depend on) rituals and routine to stay organized.

Many NeuroDivergent people have measurable, and even "diagnosable" difficulties in dealing with change.

Some of us need routine and stability. Creating chaos and instability in our day, by making us start out with change first thing in the morning is a lot to ask, and could get you in to trouble for an ADA violation because, NeuroDivergent people may have different needs, for example with Autistic people, specifically we often have a medically defined "insistence on sameness or inflexible adherence to routines, or ritualized patterns of verbal or non-verbal behavior (e.g., extreme distress at small changes, difficulties with transitions, rigid thinking patterns, greeting rituals, need to take the same route or eat the same food every day).

> **This is a medical need.** Though I don't love medical language, it does provide protections, and legal grounds for NeuroDivergent people to ask for support in work and public spaces.

If you don't accommodate all NeuroDivergent People, you may be liable for violating disability laws.

Ask yourself:

> ❖ How are you accommodating the NeuroDivergent need for sameness and routine, while still supporting employees who do need novelty and change to stay engaged?

> ❖ If hot-desking is the norm in your office, can you create a specific area where people who don't want to move to have a dedicated space they can claim as their own, and know will not be used by someone else?

Dress Codes

Are overly stringent dress codes keeping (or chasing) NeuroDivergent workers away from your workforce?

I never feel myself when my hair is not a bright and vibrant color, in fact, when my hair is dull, I feel very dull myself. If you look at the faces in the NeuroDivergent community, you'll see that many of us have bright, beautiful, eccentric, hair or dressing styles.

Relaxed dress codes are wonderful. However, to avoid the difficulty that unspoken expectations can create for NeuroDivergent employees, if there are exceptions to when and what people can wear in your workplace, it is important to document them clearly.

Be specific.

Instead of using terms like "business casual" or "business attire" give specific examples of what is and is not acceptable within your workplace.

For example, "jeans are okay as long as they do not have stains or holes in them" or "please do not wear shirts with profanity, explicit imagery, or that promote drugs and alcohol". This type of language prevents confusion and misunderstandings for people who may not easily understand social categorizations and constructs, by giving them the more specific information they need.

Surprise & Last-Minute Meetings

Not everyone loves surprises. In fact, NeuroDivergent people and people with anxiety may struggle more than others with surprises.

Respect the needs of your employees who are less spontaneous by announcing activities and sharing details related to team events in advance.

Avoiding Workplace Meltdowns

In the section about I mentioned that some NeuroDivergent people have a medically defined need for stability, that is protected by disability laws in most countries. I also shared that it has been noted in the diagnostic criteria for Autistic people (one NeuroType of many) that we "may experience extreme distress at small changes, and difficulty with transitions".

When confronted with surprises and change, we can become overwhelmed, which might manifest as meltdowns or shutdowns.

These neurological events are often exhausting, with effects lasting for hours, days, or even weeks later if the meltdown is bad enough.

Changes and surprises that often triggered my meltdowns at work were things like:

❖ People forcing me into last minute meetings.

❖ People expecting me to drop whatever I'm currently doing, without warning, and quickly shift gears to a new task that's nothing like the task I had just been doing.

❖ Managers and shift leaders changing my work end time, without giving notice to me in advance, forcing me to stay later than previously agreed upon. Usually, by the time they told me I wouldn't be able to go home at the time I had rationed my energy for, it was too late to adjust, and I would still be out of energy by my previously expected end time.

I actually CAN handle change, but it is harder for me (and many NeuroDivergent people) than it is for NeuroTypical people. Because of that, I need more time and space to handle and process change.

When confronted with new information, or a change of plans, I need time for everything to sink in, as I accept the new path that's been laid before me.

A lot of the time the world, and the people in it seems chaotic to me, so planning out my day, workload, and life, are how I create my own oasis of calm in this wild world.

The Perils of Mandatory Fun

Neurodivergent employees may not enjoy the same types of activities that NeuroTypical employees might like doing for fun.

Some environments that can help to recharge your more socially driven team members, may be draining for those who need to recharge in a calmer, solitary, or laid back, environment.

Happy hours in crowded bars and restaurants can be overwhelming, and uncomfortable, for people with sensory or auditory processing differences.

"No." means NO.

Don't make "fun activities" mandatory and avoid statements that might guilt trip or single out more introverted or less socially inclined employees like, "It's not mandatory but who wouldn't want to go to _____."

Always give employees the option to easily skip out on office social functions. Don't guilt trip people into attending organizational events.

If people decline invites to come out with the team, accept it, and don't pressure them to attend.

Talk to the people who don't want to attend events, find out what they would be able to show up for, and include those in the company activities too.

Recruiting, Hiring, & Onboarding Neurodivergent Team Members

Hiring NeuroDivergent Talent

NeuroDivergent employees are eagerly to enter the workplace, bringing along fresh perspectives and valuable skills. However, while many organizations recognize the need for and importance of employing diverse team members, the traditional hiring process frequently makes it difficult for NeuroDivergent workers to get a foot in the door.

Employers are often unfamiliar with the unique ways in which NeuroDivergent people process the world around them and interact with others, and this can lead to miscommunications and misunderstandings during the interview process.

Many NeuroDivergent individuals report not knowing how to sell themselves in an interview, due to their varied and information processing styles.

Neurodivergent is different, not broken.

In a genuinely non-discriminatory environment, your hiring process would be so inclusive that you will not need someone to disclose a diagnosis for your interview to be fair.

At the same time, in most countries, employers **are required** to provide reasonable accommodations during the hiring process **if requested**.

Your mindset should not be based on **segregation**—"NeuroDivergent people" vs. "NeuroTypical people."

NeuroDivergent individuals (and everyone else) will pick up on this, causing you to lose valuable candidates.

It is up to leaders in the organization to ensure that the Hiring & Recruiting process is fair for all candidates, NeuroTypical and NeuroDivergent alike.

Where Traditional Interviews Can Fall Short

Good liars are often VERY good at job interviews. Hiring someone who's good at interviews doesn't mean that you're going to hire a great employee. It just means you've found someone who's good at job interviews.

These tricksters may get onto your team and be nothing like the person they claimed to be when you initially engaged them. They may also exaggerate their personal values, or skill sets, and, when pressed, not be able to perform the tasks, and may not truly hold the values that they previously claimed to have.

Interview Shortfalls

In my experience hiring and recruiting talent, there are MANY people who are very good at manipulating the interview process, telling you exactly what they think you want to hear. In fact, that's what we're trained, when seeking work, to do!

I've also met some spectacular candidates, who did not showcase well in a traditional interview, but were exceptionally skilled and dedicated employees...and who would have done much better, had they been allowed to showcase their work in a less traditional way.

A Clearly Defined Hiring Process

Some employers like to "keep candidates on their toes" as a test to see how much they are willing to put up with, or if they "really want the job", and may try to keep their hiring process and timelines secret.

These deceptive tactics can be confusing to NeuroDivergent candidates, and are likely a turnoff for people who value honesty and trust, as they may feel manipulated and tricked, if you are intentionally withholding too much information from them.

Give an overview of your hiring process (verbally and in writing, if possible), and be upfront in explaining how long it will take. Let candidates know in advance, if possible, the types of interviews and screening techniques and tools you will be using.

If you don't have a standardized hiring process, documented in writing, this is a good time to officially define what the process looks like, so there is no confusion.

Job Descriptions

Job descriptions help employees gain a greater understanding of their role in the organization. A well-written job description will establish a solid set of expectations from employers to their employees.

When employees have a clear understanding of their responsibilities, they will work more effectively in their roles.

It may be time to review, refresh, and update your team's job descriptions.

Writing and maintaining job descriptions must be an ongoing task. Job descriptions should typically be reviewed and updated at least once per year.

> **NOTE:** If revising a current employee's job description, review the revised job description with the employee holding the position, so that the employee can give feedback and recommend changes for the revision.

Questions to ask about your process:

✢ Do you have a clearly outlined hiring process that is standardized for all candidates?

✢ Do you have this process documented in writing, so that you can share what the process will be like with potential new hires when they start this process with you?

✢ How accurate are your job descriptions?

Standard Interview Questions

Depending on the role, you may want to provide the standardized interview questions in advance, to support those who need time to process and deliver clear and accurate responses.

Approve and standardize questions and a process that you know is not discriminatory against people with different mental operating systems, disabilities, and other protected statuses.

Have multiple people review the interview questions and process that you have when interviewing for each role. Use these as a script, so that every candidate receives the same, fair, interview opportunities.

> **NOTE:** It is important to get the eyes of NeuroDivergent people, as well as people in other marginalizations, to review the questions and interview formats you are using, to prevent unintentional harm and bias from creeping into your screening process. Otherwise, you may be harming the diversity (both visible and invisible) of your organization.

In addition, it is important to have people with varied NeuroTypes and marginalisations on both the interview team, and the decision team, for their differing skills and insights.

How can you allow people to showcase their skills for you?

There are many skilled humans who are unable to communicate what they know accurately with speech on the fly, or in the ways society is used to.

Some of us need more time and space, or words can't do justice to the things we know, or the skills we have. We need to show you what we struggle to say.

Team members who struggle to express themselves in spoken or written speech—the traditional interview format—may appreciate being allowed to showcase their skills in other ways. Depending on the role you are trying to fill, you may, for example, ask the candidate if they have a portfolio of past work that they can share with you.

Some people, like me, express themselves more clearly, honestly, and accurately in writing than they are able to ever do with spoken communication.

Let the candidate tell you how they most comfortably communicate, and flex to accommodate those needs. Consider allowing people to provide their responses to you in writing (or video, or however they tell you they work best).

You may also consider offering them a paid work trial project or a skills test, something that has them doing the basic function(s) they will need to do in the role they are applying for.

Be prepared to move away from the traditional interview process, and please stop thinking of interviews as the interviewer VS the interviewee.

No More Sneaky Games

It's time to shift away from thinking of the interview as you against the candidate. You are creating a dialogue, not a fort for them to penetrate.

As recruiters, we need to ask ourselves: "Can the candidate perform the basic functions required of the job?" **NOT** "Were they anxious in the interview?" or "Is this going to be my new best work friend?"

It is important to focus on job skills and organizational values (like honesty, accountability, and trust). If you want honest employees, set the standard by being honest with potential new hires, being as transparent as possible, to help the candidate accurately determine if they will really be truly happy working for your organization.

This includes being up front with job descriptions, the wage you are offering, information about your organizational culture, promotion pipelines, and the pros and cons of working within your workplace.

Don't be the recruiter that tricks people into giving up something about themselves that you they shouldn't, or into accepting a job for lower pay than they deserve.

The right candidate for the job & the right job for the candidate

Great recruiters know that hiring is about getting the right person in the right seat.

Open and honest communication, NOT tricking people, is the best way to ensure a new employee is a good fit for the role they are applying for.

Determining if the candidate is a good fit:

❖ Are they the right fit for the role they are applying for? If not, are there better roles available?

❖ Do they have the skills needed to perform the job duties? OR could the candidate develop the missing skills within a reasonable amount of time?

❖ Are the candidate's professional values in line with the organizational goals and values (A professional skills based fit NOT "social culture or personality fit")?

❖ Have you been fully honest & transparent with the candidate so they can make an informed decision on whether they think they can really be happy and effective within your work environment?

Cautions on Hiring for "Culture Fit"

Diverse teams, perspectives, ideas and opinions are essential for organizational success.

When reviewing potential applicants, it is important to find team members who:

- ✥ Share the organization's beliefs

- ✥ Are suited to their tasks

- ✥ Will thrive within the organization

Unfortunately, in some organizations, culture fit can become a tool to enforce sameness, excluding differences and people who stand out or "don't fit in" for various (often unspoken) reasons.

When "Culture Fit" Harms

As I detailed earlier, I have worked for employers who used the idea of culture fit to hire, fire, and shut down people for attracting too much of the wrong kind of attention (and those who failed to conform to social norms within a work group).

The people who were let go without reason were often said to have been a "poor culture fit".

In hindsight many of the people I saw let go over the years for being a "bad culture fit" were really dismissed for showing too many obvious NeuroDivergent traits:

✤ Being "socially awkward" or "too talkative"

✤ Being "easily distracted"

✤ Making sounds and noises while working

✤ Not "getting it" or "struggling to understand unspoken office rules"

✤ Struggling to "fit in"

Unconscious Bias Against NeuroDivergent People

Often with NeuroDiversity, as with other forms of diversity, our unconscious biases can cause great unintended harm and consequences to those we are biased against.

An organization's culture, if set up incorrectly, or if it is allowed to become unhealthy, may be harmful, and can even violate anti-discrimination laws.

If your culture is based on social aspects, such as how well you all get along with each other, and what bars you like to visit on Fridays, it may exclude people who fall outside of those norms, or are uncomfortable in those environments and types of social situations.

If in your organization "culture fit" has grown to mean hiring more people who think, look, and act just like the existing members of the organization, your organization may be leaving itself open to litigation.

This is why it can be better not to look for culture fit, but instead to focus on finding a skills and values fit, seeking out employees who embody your organizational values. Helping to avoid discriminating against people based on their personal beliefs, NeuroType, lifestyle, and other differences that have nothing to do with the quality of work they can do.

Transparency is Crucial for people with Disabilities & Appreciated by Everyone

Believe it or not, if you think the person is not going to be satisfied working in that position or for your company, the best thing you can do is to let them know the parts of their job you think they may not like, so that they can make an educated decision on if they're up for whatever those potential obstacles may be.

This is especially true for people with disabilities, to accurately answer the job interview question "Can you perform the job's required duties with or without reasonable accommodation?"

It is an employer's legal obligation to provide any person with a disability reasonable accommodation under the ADA (Americans with Disabilities Act).

If you are asking people to perform more than the "essential functions' that are in a person's job description, and you are not transparent and clear with all requirements and duties, or your job description is inaccurate, you may be exposing yourself to a lawsuit.

Hiring someone, and hiding the less desirable truths from them during your initial engagements, may also feel like a bait and switch, and can lead to employee turnover.

Turnover can be an expensive loss—sometimes more than the cost of a person's annual salary, when you consider the loss in training and onboarding, the moral dips that happen when team members leave (which is harder to quantify), and the time and cost of rehiring someone for the role.

Also, don't try to trick people into taking the lowest pay you can give them for a role. Do your research and set what the role is worth to you IN ADVANCE, before meeting or screening any candidates. To avoid bias, try not to change that number after you start interviewing.

I recommend sharing the pay in your job postings publicly, or at the beginning of the process, being fully transparent whenever possible.

YOUR part as the employer—Questions to Ask:

❖ Do you promise to make the interview, onboarding, and employment process safe, fair, and flexible to support all candidates?

❖ Is your organization transparent in outlining its hiring process, sharing expectations from the beginning, letting candidates know how long the application process will take, and informing them of the steps for that process in advance?

❖ Are the Job postings for this organization accurate, concise, and written in easy-to-understand language that only includes essential qualities for the job the candidate is applying for?

❖ Do you only ask for skills that are needed to do the essential functions of the job?

❖ Are the questions in your current process possibly ILLEGAL or discriminatory, leaving your company at risk of litigation?

Onboarding: The Value of Proper Training/Education for ALL Team Members

Onboarding & Support for Neurodivergent Employees

Once an organization manages to acquire talent, proper **Onboarding & Training** become essential **for any new hire's success** (whether NeuroDivergent or NeuroTypical).

NeuroDivergent employees may need more support in this initial startup period, and **without help**, have an **increased risk** of becoming turnover, especially **during the first 90 days of employment**.

New situations can be stressful for some NeuroDivergent brains, so the more up front clarity you can provide for new hires the better, allowing team members to more easily settle into their new roles and routines.

Some information you might consider sharing the first day may include:

❖ An itinerary for the first week (at least)

❖ A checklist of assignments and goals for the first week (at least)

❖ Important contact information for other team members, leaders, mentors, and people the new hire may need to reach to coordinate and collaborate on job duties

If we think of our new employees as plants:

Our plants will need extra care and proper support in the first few months, as they begin to grow a foundation, laying roots within the company.

Proper training, onboarding, and support for NeuroDivergent Employees, from managers and teammates, **during this crucial startup period** can significantly **reduce the risk of NeuroDivergent (and NeuroTypical) turnover.**

We can do this by equipping new team members with the right tools for success as we welcome them into their new roles within our organizations.

These tools may include but are not limited to:

❖ Accurate and clearly defined and up to date job descriptions

❖ Well-written, accessible employee handbooks

❖ Supportive trainers and mentors that can cater training to the different learning styles of the people they teach

Employees may benefit from professional and personal growth opportunities, such as:

❖ One-on-one coaching

❖ Development sessions

❖ Regular check-ins during the onboarding process or job and organizational transitions

Supportive Trainers and Mentors

Pay extra attention to the initial onboarding process. NeuroDivergent people may need extra time to settle in and complete any initial training.

If you generally give new employees a month or two to settle in, it may take a bit longer for new NeuroDivergent team members, who may need additional time to acclimate to new job duties. The same goes for when an existing NeuroDivergent employee is transitioning to a new role within the same company, when there has been a change in manager, location, software or job role, including (and especially) a promotion.

The same goes for when an existing NeuroDivergent employee is transitioning to a new role within the same company. The employee may need additional time to acclimate to new job duties.

Questions to Ask:

❖ Are managers, mentors, and trainers **regularly checking in** with new hires throughout the **crucial startup process**?

❖ Is the training being tailored to the **individual learner's needs**?

❖ As part of the process, has **Assistive Technology** been considered?

What is Assistive Technology?

Assistive technologies enhance people's lives by allowing people with disabilities (both visible and invisible) to perform functions that might otherwise be difficult or impossible for them.

Autism

Because I'm Autistic myself, I've shared many examples of Autistic accommodations throughout this book. However, a few additional ideas are below.

Technological Options:

✤ **Visual Organizational and project planning applications** (such as TIIMO, Google Calendar or another visual schedule, Evernote, etc.)

✤ **Headphones** with music, noise canceling, or white noise to control sensory input.

✤ **Text-to-speech software** that reads typed items so the user can have an alternative method of communication if they are situationally or entirely non-speaking, or a way of taking in text if they struggle with following the written (and typed) word.

✤ **Speech-to-text/dictation software** allows a person to dictate notes and information by quickly converting spoken words to text. This be helpful if writing by hand is difficult or creates an obstacle. Allowing someone who struggles with handwriting to type. Not requiring handwriting can also be beneficial for those who struggle with differences in motor control.

✤ **Smartphones and tablets** often include many of the desired technology above, allowing users to take their accessible tech wherever they go.

Low Tech Options:

✤ Provide written instructions over spoken directions.

✤ Give instructions as written numbered lists or checklists to help with task tracking.

✤ Use visual aids, such as visible schedules, prompts, and written reminders for deadlines, meetings, and expectations.

✤ Try to avoid unspoken expectations. For many reasons, it is essential to have a written employee handbook with well-outlined policies and procedures clearly defined in writing.

✤ When explaining projects and work concepts, it may be helpful to explain in detail how things work and why things are done the way they are, rather than telling people what they are expected to do without sharing why.

✤ Don't forget about the sensory environment!

ADHD

Technological Options:

❖ **Organizational and project planning applications** (such as TIIMO, Inflow, Droptask, Asana, Evernote, Rescue Time, etc.).

❖ **Headphones** with music, noise canceling, or white noise to block out distractions.

❖ **Text-to-speech software** that reads written materials so the user can take in information through the ears instead of through the eyes if it helps with attention/or if it is challenging to be attentive when reading.

❖ **Scanners** (hand and desktop) that allow a user to scan and then listen to the text found in physical books and other non-digitized media if it helps with attention/or if it is challenging to be attentive when reading. Similarly, **Smartpens** can record both writing and audio, translating written or spoken notes into typed notes.

❖ **Speech-to-text/dictation software** (to manage executive functioning) allows a person to dictate notes and information by quickly converting spoken words to text. This can be vital when combined with word processors, notepads, timers, task lists, and other reminders.

❖ **Spell and grammar checkers** to help find errors and correct problems, misspellings, and typos within written communications if they find proofreading or attention to detail difficult.

Low Tech Options:

❖ Offer help prioritizing tasks, and be sure to break large projects down, giving the smaller pieces of the project clear deadlines, building up to the completion of the final project.

❖ Provide bulletin boards, note pads, sticky notes, task lists, and desktop calendars to jot quick thoughts on to keep them safe without interrupting workflows.

❖ Allow employees to have working periods where they can focus on tasks without being interrupted by other team members.

❖ Be sure every task has a written due date, and provide lists of tasks with due dates when applicable.

❖ Try to place ADHDers in tasks they enjoy and are well suited for whenever possible. ADHDers may find tedious or mundane tasks hard to grasp because they may be painfully boring (literally), meaning they may excel at more complex functions that hold their attention more easily.

Dyscalculia

Technological Options:

❖ Have calculators readily available for anyone who needs them.

❖ **Speech-to-text/dictation software** allows a person to dictate notes and information by quickly converting spoken words to text.

✤ **Maps & GPS** can be beneficial for people who struggle to remember directions if driving or traveling is part of their job description.

✤ **Digital Clocks** can be easier for some people with Dyscalculia to read than analogue clocks.

Low Tech Options:

✤ If math is not in the job description of a person with Dyscalculia, don't ask or force them to do the math. If math is in their job description, you might consider if it HAS to be. If not, ask that individual if removing unnecessary math-related duties would make their lives easier and less stressful.

✤ Provide **notepads** for people who struggle to remember numbers such as phone numbers, zip codes, or other numbers used around the workplace.

✤ Allow those who struggle in math to pair up with skilled people in this area if working on a project requiring mathematical calculations.

Dyslexia

Technological Options:

✤ **Text-to-speech software** that reads written materials so the user can take in information through the ears instead of through the eyes.

✤ **Speech-to-text/dictation software** allows a person to dictate notes and information by quickly converting spoken words to text.

✤ **Scanners** (hand and desktop) that allow a user to scan and then listen to the text found in physical books and other non-digitized media.

✤ **Spell and grammar checkers** to help find errors and correct problems, misspellings, and typos within written communications.

✤ **Smart pens** can record both writing and audio, translating written or spoken notes into typed notes.

Low Tech Options:

✤ Show examples of desired work product outcomes to help set clear expectations.

✤ Providing materials on colored papers or overlays can make it easier for people with Dyslexia to read without errors. Font style and font size can also have an impact on reading.

Dyspraxia/Apraxia

Technological Options:

✤ Allow the use of word processors and other technology if handwriting is difficult.

✤ **Speech-to-text/dictation software** allows a person to dictate notes and information by quickly converting spoken words to text.

NOTE: If we embrace the software and tools that automatically make certain types of corrections for us, such as handwriting, grammar, and typing speeds (once cherished workplace skills) are quickly made irrelevant.

Low Tech Options:

✤ Allow the employee to work in "non-traditional" positions, such as (but not limited to) leaning, laying on the floor, feet in the chair, standing, etc.

✤ Provide a tiltable/adjustable height and angle working service that can adjust to the individual's needs.

✤ Provide pencil and pen grips or specialized writing tools, such as gel pens and other smooth ink pens that are less sensitive to the user's writing pressure.

✤ Allow extra time for new tasks requiring physical coordination and movements.

✤ Allow to work while sitting when reasonable, and provide anti-fatigue mats, grab bars, padded edges for sharp corners, and other protective gear when appropriate.

Apraxia of Speech

Making space for people to communicate in ways other than spoken speech is vital. Ensure these communicators are heard, understood, and represented in meetings and the organization.

Technological Options:

✤ **Text-to-speech software** that turns the user's written communication into a computerized spoken voice so that the user can communicate information to people who communicate using spoken words.

✤ Augmentative and Alternative Communication (ACC) Devices for communicating without speech, such as an app (with or without speech generation, on the user's iPad, mobile phone, or laptop).

Low Tech Options:

✤ Low Tech AAC: sign language, communication books, symbol boards, and choice cards (to name a few).

✤ Provide written notes for tasks/projects.

Hyperlexia

Technological Options:

✤ **Spell and grammar checkers** to help find errors and correct problems, misspellings, and typos within written communications.

✤ **Organizational and project planning applications** (such as TIIMO, Inflow, Droptask, Asana, Evernote, Rescue Time, etc.)

Low Tech Options:

✤ Provide written instructions over spoken directions.

✤ Give instructions as written numbered lists or checklists to help with task tracking.

❖ Use visual aids, such as visible schedules, prompts, and written reminders for deadlines, meetings, and expectations.

❖ For many reasons, it is essential to have a written employee handbook with well-outlined policies and procedures clearly defined in writing.

❖ Show examples of desired work product outcomes to help set clear expectations.

Obsessive Compulsive Disorder

Technological Options:

❖ **Organizational and project planning applications** (such as TIIMO, Inflow, Droptask, Asana, Evernote, Rescue Time, etc.) if there are difficulties in this area.

❖ **Headphones** with music, noise canceling, or white noise can help to create a soothing, relaxing environment.

❖ Technology that allows work from home or taking meetings virtually (if doing so would benefit the employee's mental health).

❖ Anxiety, stress, and mental health management apps.

Low Tech Options:

❖ Appropriate training for managers about working with people who have OCD and similar mental health conditions.

❖ Flexible schedule with time off and breaks as needed.

✤ Additional time to complete tasks.

✤ Allow them to have their own space.

Tourettes & Tics

Technological Options:

✤**Headphones** with music, noise canceling, or white noise to block out distractions or other tic triggers.

✤Anxiety, stress, and mental health management apps - as stress and anxiety can increase tics.

.

Low Tech Options:

✤Appropriate training for managers and other employees about Tourettes and tics.

✤Allow them to work in environments with minimal distractions.

✤Flexible schedule with time off and breaks as needed.

Don't forget the two T's (time & training)!

Just like with any other new system that an organization implements; it is vital that you provide training and support to those who will be using assistive technology within your workplaces.

Additionally, it is important to give a new AT user time to get acquainted with and learn how to use their new technology.

"Because I said So" won't Work for Some People

For example, something that I, and many NeuroDivergent people, need during onboarding is clarity around how things actually work and the "why" behind the tasks we are being asked to complete.

If you were to simply tell me that I need to do something, without explaining the reason behind a task to me, it is less likely that I will remember the instruction that I've been given.

I am a person who's always been driven by the question "Why?"

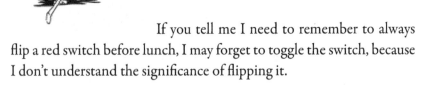

If you tell me I need to remember to always flip a red switch before lunch, I may forget to toggle the switch, because I don't understand the significance of flipping it.

However, if you were to tell me that flipping the switch feeds lunch to the office pet, and me doing so will make sure an animal won't starve, and then show me the animal who needs to eat, and how the red switch feeds it, I am much more likely to remember (because I understand the importance of doing so).

The Importance of Documentation

All employees need some form of **guidance as a foundation** to understand their roles within an organization.

Organizational Rules, help team members understand the values and goals with which they should operate within a workplace (helping to keep everyone in alignment with the organizational events and practices).

Rules, Policies, & Procedures outline what leadership an organization expects from its employees and should be **specific, clear, and as simple as possible**. This clarity is even more critical for NeuroDivergent employees, with communication and processing differences, who may not pick up on less explicit, unwritten rules and expectations.

If policies are unclear, employees may not understand the expectations placed upon them by other organization members.

Without **well-documented rules, Policies, & Procedures**, employees are likely to **waste valuable time** and energy figuring out **how** things are supposed to be done instead of focusing on their assigned tasks.

In addition, some organizational **Rules, Policies, & Procedures** can cause harm to your NeuroDivergent team members, while well thought out and documented **Rules, Policies, & Procedures** can help people with diverse minds to thrive.

Beware of Unspoken Rules & Expectations

Though it's great to be in sync, unspoken expectations can cause confusion organization-wide. You may even have some "unwritten rules" within your organization.

Rules that are implied or unsaid can be especially confusing to NeuroDivergent people.

It's also possible that some team members are feeling as if the leader(s) sometimes expects their direct reports to know what they are thinking or read their mind(s).

Put it in Writing

Improper documentation can be damaging to your organizational health and morale. NeuroDivergent team members are at increased risk when expectations aren't made clear.

Employee Handbook

Everything should be clearly documented in your organization's Employee Handbook, or you may have people unintentionally breaking organizational policy and procedure, but have no idea that they are making mistakes, because they have never been told in a way that sticks.

If your organization does not have a handbook, or if the handbook is not current or out of date, it's past time for your organization to ensure this is corrected.

If you do have an employee handbook, be sure it is kept up to date and that everyone on the team knows about it, including where they can easily access the document and who they can speak to should they have any further questions.

Keep Your Handbook Up to Date

❖ At least once a year, get the leaders of your organization together to review your Employee Handbook and brainstorm if any rules or expectations have changed.

❖ Ask organizational leaders to be observant, and ask them to identify any unwritten rules or any unspoken expectations they notice, or have personally.

❖ Also brainstorm with your team regarding the things that are expected by people, but are not written down, not talked about, or not typically shared with new employees.

❖ Start documenting and writing things down. Make it explicitly clear what those expectations are.

How Leaders can Support NeuroDivergent Employees

There are certain types of leaders who don't mix well with many of my NeuroDivergent traits and tendencies.

Back when I was an assistant manager at a fast-food restaurant in high school, at the age of 17, I used to think leadership was about having people around you do what you tell them.

Now, as a more seasoned leader, I realize that it's the leader's job to serve the people they lead.

My job as a leader is to support my team, solve problems with them, work alongside them, and help to remove obstacles that prevent them from reaching their goals.

Leadership isn't about the leader. Without a team there is no need for the leader—and a leader is nothing without a team.

In leadership I no longer look for obedience. I work to earn the trust and respect of the people I work with. I don't expect respect-based titles, and I always encourage the people I support as a leader to speak honestly and transparently with me, even if they need to tell me I've done something wrong.

If we all are able to respect and trust each other, as we are working together towards a common goal, obedience is not necessary, because team members can instead focus on what they believe is best for the organization and their team.

Communication with Leaders

Within an organization, there are many types of communication differences, beyond visual or audio communication methods.

Quick to Speak & Act or More Cautious?

There are communicators who are quick to speak, think, and react, in conversation, while others need more time to reflect and process details—seeming to respond on a delay, when compared to their more spontaneous peers.

Detail Oriented or High Level?

There are detail-oriented people, who need as much information as possible to make decisions, or before they can speak on a topic.

There are also high-level overview people, who may find too many details to be overwhelming.

Neither way is wrong, and both styles of work have value and contribute to teams in varied ways.

Both those who make quick decisions, and those who compile facts and data to make accurate decisions, are important.

Sometimes a quick decision must be made, and other decisions require careful analysis. Building a team with both of these traits nurtured and encouraged, is one way to ensure ALL your employees thrive.

Direct or Soft Communicators?

Within any space, you will likely have communicators who are very direct, and like to cut to the point.

NeuroDivergent people often can be very direct communicators.

In contrast to that, and often confusing to me, personally, as an NeuroDivergent person, are communicators who are less direct.

Making Space for Varied Communication Input and Output

Good leaders understand the nuances and differences in the human communication spectrum, and know how to support, mediate, and hold space for all types of communication within their organization: direct, indirect, quick speaking, delayed processors, those who use spoken word, written communication, or ACC.

Make accommodating people with varied communication needs and preferences a standard process, by offering information in writing for those who work better in text, and offering to talk through directions if people prefer spoken communication.

> **NOTE:** Leaders in the organization should be willing to provide instructions or meeting minutes in writing, if requested, and allow people the time and space to take notes and respond if needed.

Performance Reviews, Feedback, & Guidance

Everyone within your organization will benefit from regular performance reviews and feedback meetings with Leadership, provided clear guidance and helpful feedback is offered.

Regular check-ins and reviews help members of an organization to better understand how their goals relate to the organization's larger goals.

It can also be helpful to encourage team members to share feedback on how they communicate best, how people can best communicate and work with them, or if they feel meetings and your processes could be better or more inclusive.

Goals help align members of an organization with the company's mission. They also help employees see how their individual contributions fit into the bigger picture of the workplace as a whole.

Regular check-in meetings between managers and employees keeps dialogue open, so that managers are available to help discuss and remove any obstacles or challenges that may prevent an employee from reaching their goals, once set.

With clear, actionable, and well thought out goals in place, it can help to align teams, steering them more effectively in the direction of the organization's larger goals.

Don't forget: When leaders are assigning tasks, be sure to let team members know, or let them ask, when a task needs to be completed, and ensure that everyone involved in a project or task understands all checkpoints and deadlines.

Clear, well-defined goals can help organizational efforts, and increase the chances of achieving your team's individual and organizational goals.

Realistic, Clearly Defined, Measurable Goals for Setting Clear Expectation

To avoid confusion and improve organizational efficiency, managers and team members should work together to set specific goals that are measurable, so that team members can easily tell if they are on track or not.

Your individual and organizational goals should be realistic, clearly defined, and measurable:

♣ **Realistic**: When you set organizational goals that are so high they cannot be reached, it eventually can destroy the morale of your employees. This is why it is important to create realistic goals for your team members.

> Also, before assigning a goal to someone, it is a good idea to ask them **if they feel the goal is possible in the allotted amount of time**, with the current available resources—and if not, how can the goal be supported, or changed, to be more realistic?

Set expectations by creating a reasonable, practical, and timely deadline for each goal—including checkpoints. This is also part of creating realistic goals.

♣ **Providing team members with a realistic deadline** for when they should have reached their goal can help them to correctly plan, monitor, and eventually reach them.

❖ **Clearly defined**, with specific information, what you expect of each person, including the tasks they need to do, and when the work should be finished by.

Having clearly defined goals for the organization, teams, and individual contributors will make it more likely people are able to accomplish what is expected of them

Consider such questions as:

❖ What needs to be accomplished?

❖ Why is this goal important to the organization or team?

❖ How will this be accomplished? Are there any special rules or parameters for this task?

❖ What teams, leaders, or other resources will be involved or need to be accounted for during this project?

❖ **Measurable:** The goals you set should have clearly measurable outcomes, allowing members of the organization to gauge their progress towards their goal, and easily know if their goals are off track, and assess their own progress.

> **Are your goals quantifiable?** If not, it is important to develop criteria for measuring people's progress towards their individual and team goals.

> **What measurable outcomes** can you use for your unique organizational needs?

> **It is important to agree on a realistic deadline** for a goal to be met by specifying how you will know and measure when a goal has been completed.

For example: Will you increase sales or productivity by a certain percent? What is a realistic number, considering the timeline and skill pool?

As managers and organizational leaders, it is important that we help set, check in, guide, and remove obstacles that keep the members of the organization from reaching their goals.

Regular Check-Ins are Key

> **IMPORTANT:** After setting goals, it is crucial for leaders to have regular check-ins with team members regarding their goals, so that problems can be addressed right away, as soon as an employee becomes aware of them, and notifies their manager that their goals are in danger of becoming, or have become, off track.

Also important for this, is that the employee trusts their manager enough to be honest with them.

Benefits that NeuroDivergent Employees (and NeuroTypicals) Want & Need

There are certain benefits that are crucial to the success and empowerment of NeuroDivergent people within workplaces. Many of these benefits are things that everyone in your organization likely wants and will benefit from.

As I say frequently, when we give everyone access to the things NeuroDivergent people need, it can help make society better for everyone, including NeuroTypical people.

A Living Wage

The first benefit that NeuroDivergent people (and all people) need in order to be successful is a living wage.

> **NOTE:** a living wage is NOT the same as minimum wage. A living wage means an amount that can adequately allow your employee (and their family if they have one) a "normal" standard of living (having enough shelter, food, etc).

This one may seem like a no-brainer, however many NeuroDivergent people report being under or unemployed.

Living in a state of poverty, constantly worrying if you will be able to pay all your bills, keep a roof over your head, survive on your own, or be able to eat, takes a toll on a person's mental resources. As does having to work multiple jobs, just to try and cover those needs.

People need to have all of their basic needs met, if they are going to thrive in life, the world, the workplace and beyond.

Historically, marginalized peoples have struggled with acquiring fair wages, with many living below the poverty line. Employees who don't have their needs met may struggle to show up fully present, and as their best selves, to your workplaces, because they may be worried about other things happening outside of work.

Flexible Schedules

When speaking to NeuroDivergent people online, one of the most asked for benefits has been the ability to have more control over their own schedules.

There are multiple reasons many of us need additional control over our schedules. One reason being that NeuroDivergent productivity can wax and wane, with periods of hyperfocus and creative crashes. Some of us struggle with insomnia, and others report being productive at varied times of day.

The ability of an employee to custom tailor their schedule around their individual needs, means employees can work when they are at their best, thus maximizing their skills and productivity.

It's good for EVERYONE!

Like with other changes organizations can make that empower their NeuroDivergent staff, flexible schedules can be helpful to everyone within your organization.

For example, parents and caregivers, regardless of NeuroType, can benefit from flexible schedules that allow them to work around the needs of their loved ones, appointments, and other obligations.

Ability to Work Remotely

As a person with sensory processing differences, I am only physically comfortable when I have almost complete control over my sensory environment. This means I am uncomfortable almost every time I leave my home and enter a public space.

If I undergo overexposure to my sensory triggers, I may experience disorientation, vertigo, migraines, and even seizures. Avoiding sensory triggers is essential to my health and ability to function as needed in work and other areas of my life.

Working from home means I am able to work efficiently, in an environment that I have been able to tailor perfectly to my needs. I am able to do a better job and get more work done, because I am working when and where I am at my best.

My sensory differences also mean that, though I am able to drive, doing so is difficult for me, especially during heavy traffic times (like rush hour) when people are heading to and from work.

Seizures and epilepsy are also more common in NeuroDivergent brains.

Because, at the time of writing this book, I have been seizure free for well over two years, I am permitted to drive a vehicle. However, those who have more frequent seizures, or who have had recent seizures, may be unable to drive.

In some cases, having seizures and other neurological events will prevent governing bodies from issuing a driver's license, or can result in revoking the license of an individual.

You may be missing out on top talent

Requiring people to physically be present in an office, when work can just as easily be done from home, means missing out on many talented candidates.

Regardless of the reason (medical need or personal preference), allowing people who can benefit from working remotely to do so, is empowering people to work in ways that are most efficient and comfortable for them.

Guilt Free Personal Time Off, Sick Pay, Mental Health Days, FMLA

One of the number one benefits that NeuroDivergent people (and many NeuroTypicals) both want and need for is a fair and flexible PTO policy, and an environment where taking PTO is not met with guilt.

> **NOTE:** There are many different types of PTO policies. For more information outlining the pros and cons of some of the most common types of time off, please see the section titled "".

People should be encouraged and able to take advantage of the PTO they have.

It is important to monitor PTO, and have discussions with your team about scheduling their time off, especially if you notice a team member not taking time or accumulating time off that they aren't using. These discussions may highlight potential staffing or cultural issues within your organization.

Why Team Members May Not Take Their PTO

Some employees may not feel able to take time off if doing so will cause them more stress: for example, if they are worried that all of their tasks won't be taken care of while they are out of the office.

Some team members may know their tasks can be taken care of, but may not want to burden their coworkers with their workload so they can take time off.

That's why, whenever possible, every person, task, or role within your organization should have at least one (preferably multiple) backups, in case someone has a sudden need to be away from work or takes PTO.

Regardless of what PTO policy you choose, it is important to ensure you are not understaffed and that every role has at least two people (sometimes more, depending on the volume of work) who are capable of completing the tasks in any given role.

Otherwise, your employees may struggle to "turn work off" and relax in their rest time, which is counterproductive to the actual goal of PTO: recharging oneself.

> **NOTE**: this means not employing just enough workers to cover the exact tasks required, provided everyone is present and nothing goes wrong. Consider that employing more workers will result in less stress, and fewer missed deadlines, making your employees much more able to be their best selves.

Follow the Leader

Leaders within the organization should be mindful of setting good examples of work life balance, by not overworking and taking time off.

Employees, regardless of brain type, tend to follow the examples of organizational leadership. If the leaders of an organization model unhealthy work habits and regularly work excessive hours and fail to take PTO, then employees may take cues from their leaders, and assume that working around the clock without rest ais expected, whether this is true or not.

Shortened Work Weeks/Shorter Work Days (25-30 hours)

Some NeuroDivergent people may not be able to handle a forty-hour work week, or may be able to handle more or less hours, depending on the types of tasks they are completing.

Needing to work less hours doesn't necessarily mean the person will get less work done, as often the hours NeuroDivergent people do work (when properly supported and not overworked) can be highly focused and productive (depending on the task), especially if the person is able to maximize their ability to work when and where they are at their best.

The Type of Task Matters

✤ **Energizing Tasks:** these are tasks that are well suited to our skills and abilities. Tasks we know well, and tasks that we enjoy, can be energizing. This helps to keep us motivated, as well as keeping our energy levels up, meaning we may be able to work for more hours.

✤ **Draining Tasks:** these are tasks that are poor matches for our skill sets, tasks we are in the early stages of learning, or tasks that we hate. These types of tasks drain our energy and motivation, meaning we will get tired faster and need to rest sooner, or stack energizing tasks in with the draining tasks to balance things out.

This is true for all humans regardless of brain type, but even more true for NeuroDivergent brains, that can be highly specialized, and may struggle with things NeuroTypicals take for granted.

ADHDers, for example, may struggle with and find "mundane", "simple", "tedious" and "boring" tasks, or "the easy things" to be more difficult and draining than "harder", "complex tasks", that require more attention and focus—which give our energy seeking brains something stimulating to latch onto.

Respecting People's Available Energy

In addition to making sure people are well suited to, have the skills for, and enjoy the work they do, we must learn to respect people's available energy—and that this availability will fluctuate.

Some of us have more energy to give than others, or may need more recharge time between activates, depending on many factors, and this is not limited to NeuroDivergent people.

Health Insurance

When I asked my NeuroDivergent audience on social media about the workplace benefits they want and need, decent health insurance was one of the first things many of them mentioned.

Because NeuroDivergence often runs in families, and NeuroDivergent people often have co-occurring health conditions in addition to being NeuroDivergent, many of my readers prioritized having affordable healthcare for themselves and their partner(s) and offspring.

NeuroDiversity and Gender Affirming Care

Options for NeuroDiversity affirming care providers are important for NeuroDivergent families, and since NeuroDivergent people are also more likely to be transgender or gender nonconforming, having insurance that covers gender affirming care was a priority to many of my readers.

Retirement Options

Every human on earth will eventually have to retire from the workplace, and when that happens, we all want to know that we will still be able to survive even past when we are able to work.

People with disabilities, both visible and invisible are often painfully aware of how fragile the balance of life and health can be.

Your employees, both NeuroDivergent and NeuroTypical, crave the security that comes with knowing that they one day will be able to stop working, and enjoy their retirement, when the appropriate time comes.

Where is the love?

Treating people like machines instead of living breathing people won't cut it in the workplace of the future.

Employees are dedicating large portions of their lives to their employers, but what happens when an employee can no longer work?

Will they be cast aside and forgotten, like disposable objects, once they're no longer of use?

There are many different types of retirement plans[1], pensions, and options available to you as the employer. If you do not choose to offer retirement options to your employees, it may be sending unintended messages to your staff and potential new hires. Namely that you, as an employer, don't care about the future of your employees, or that your organization isn't one to work for long term, because there will be little to no reward for doing so VS working in a company that does offer retirement benefits.

Mentorship Programs

Many of the benefits that NeuroDivergent people want and need are actually things that many NeuroTypicals can appreciate and benefit from as well.

For example, mentorship programs can benefit everyone within an organization, regardless of NeuroType.

During the onboarding process, it can be especially helpful for new hires to have a positive workplace role model to look up to.

Everybody Wins

A mentor's job is to help their mentee grow and develop new skills, such as problem-solving and other abilities, as they get acclimated to a new work environment or role.

---

1. https://www.irs.gov/retirement-plans/plan-sponsor/types-of-retirement-plans

Mentees aren't the only ones who benefit from mentoring relationships. Team members who take the role of mentoring others can have a fantastic opportunity to practice and grow their leadership skills. Mentors also may find satisfaction in helping other people grow and thrive.

In Conclusion

True inclusion benefits everyone, and is good for business, as it leads to happier, healthier, employees and better organizational culture.

NeuroDiversity includes all brains, both NeuroDivergent and NeuroTypical. Truly NeuroDiverse organizations are a mix of many different brain types. Making spaces NeuroDiversity affirming means making them better for ALL brains.

Now that you've made it to the end of the book, you may be tempted to jump right in and start up a NeuroDiversity hiring initiative, but I caution you to start by working with your existing team before trying to bring on new talent.

Why? Because 15-20 percent of the world's population is estimated to be NeuroDivergent in some way[1]. That is potentially one in five people!

Many of us who are NeuroDivergent diverge from what is considered "average" (by our current society) in multiple ways.

We now know that there are many NeuroDivergent people in the world, however, because NeuroDiversity is an invisible form of diversity, the true percentages and types of these differences may remain hidden, until we forge a truly diverse society.

A Better Question

---

1. https://academic.oup.com/bmb/article/135/1/108/5913187?

People often ask "how can we recruit NeuroDivergent talent to our organization?" and it's not a bad question. However, there are better questions that should be asked first, such as "do we have any NeuroDivergent people on our team at the moment?" and "do those team members feel comfortable sharing that part of themselves within the organization?"

You Probably Have NeuroDivergent Team Members Already

It's likely you have NeuroDivergent people in your life and workplace at this very moment, especially if you have more than 10 employees. Some may know they are NeuroDivergent, and some may not, especially those born in and before the early 1980s (when many of these neurodevelopmental differences were poorly defined and understood).

Disclosures Can be Risky

Those who are fortunate enough to know themselves, and their NeuroTypes, may or may not decide to share this information with others.

Though disclosure can often be the key thing that leads us to having proper support in the workplace (and beyond), unfortunately doing so can be dangerous and counterproductive in an unsafe environment.

As mentioned previously, many NeuroDivergent people have had bad experiences sharing this information with others, or know the pain of being scolded when asking for help or accommodations.

After repeatedly being shut down, scolded, and dismissed, we can become closed off, hesitant to share those parts of ourselves, unless we are absolutely sure it will be beneficial and, most importantly, safe, for us to do so.

These fears are reasonable, because though some safe, truly NeuroDiversity Affirming organizations do exist, those organizations are still, sadly, in the minority.

Many organizations today, even those who claim to be safe and inclusive, continue to miss the mark when it comes to including those with invisible differences. This means NeuroDivergence, of course, but also LGBTQIA+ inclusion as well (a common intersection for NeuroDivergent brains, since people who do not identify with the sex they were assigned at birth are three to six times as likely to be autistic as cisgender people[2], according to one very large study of 641,860 people).

> **NOTE:** Another question you should ask, instead of how to recruit LGBTQIA+ people, is to ask yourself "do the LGBTQIA+ members of your team feel safe discussing that part of their identity within your workplace?"

---

2. https://www.spectrumnews.org/news/largest-study-to-date-confirms-overlap-between-autism-and-gender-diversity/

If neither group feels safe disclosing, or you feel neither group is represented within your organization, it can point at a bigger problem, and may mean you're not yet ready to bring on new talent.

Jumping In

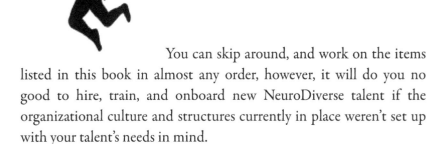

You can skip around, and work on the items listed in this book in almost any order, however, it will do you no good to hire, train, and onboard new NeuroDiverse talent if the organizational culture and structures currently in place weren't set up with your talent's needs in mind.

If your organization is in need of a tune up, and you don't fix your current issues, before bringing on new staff, you're likely wasting precious time, resources, and energy on a fruitless effort.

We've covered many topics in this book, and even if you're feeling inspired, knowing where to start can be difficult, so I'll give you a 3 tips:

1. **The most important thing is to start somewhere.** If there's an organizational problem staring you in the face, feel free to jump on that. Treat this book and its sections like an elephant that you have to "eat one bite at a time". Tackle one thing at a time, making your way through each item on the list in any order that suits you.

1. **Many people will jump straight into rewriting policies**, which is great (and may be immediately necessary), especially if bad policies and procedures are obviously harmful. Don't forget the importance of organizational culture, as many of the items listed in that section, if done poorly, can lead to poor organizational morale, NeuroDivergent exclusion, and turnover. There is a reason I've placed that section in the first half of the book, before the section about organizational policies, rules and procedures. Organizational culture doesn't HAVE to be the FIRST section you take on, but it is something that should be prioritized.

1. **If you don't know where to begin**, speaking with your leaders and team, and allowing for anonymous feedback, can be a good starting point. Be sure to check back in the section titled "" for more information on how you can kick things off within your organization.

Glossary of Terms

Note about Autistic, with autism & on the spectrum:

In this book, I have chosen to use the term "Autistic" with a capital letter "A" to describe Autistic people over "with autism", because I feel my Autistic experience is a crucial part of my human identity.

"With autism" also does not feel right to me, as it makes it sound as if autism is something I carry alongside me, like a bag or a coat, that could be left behind. Autism is such a huge part of who I am and my experience of the world that it cannot be taken away, without completely changing who I am as a person.

Not everyone feels this way, and may prefer terms such as "with autism". The best way to find out is to ensure people feel safe enough to share with you the what language they prefer.

A Spectrum is NOT Linear

Some may also say that they are "on the autism spectrum" (or use the term Autism Spectrum Disorder/Differenc, or ASD), which is fine, provided that people understand the spectrum is not linear.

When people hear that something is a spectrum, they often assume that spectrum is from high to low functioning, without understanding that the spectrum is more like a color wheel, including sensory and motor control differences, executive function and information processing differences, perception differences, and language processing and communication differences.

NeuroDivergent people can be fantastic employees, if they are empowered, equipped, and supported by those around them (especially if allowed to work on tasks well suited to their skill sets).

❖ **ADHD** (Attention-deficit/hyperactivity disorder/): Neurodevelopmental difference often diagnosed in childhood. ADHDers may express difficulties with attention, hyperactivity, and impulsiveness. ADHDers may also be creative, out of the box thinkers, who may struggle with boring, tedious, or mundane tasks, but can excel when challenged (especially if allowed to hyperfocus on a project they are passionate about).

❖ **Attentional bias:** the human tendency to pay attention to some things while simultaneously ignoring others. Attentional bias is different for every person, but may be more extreme in those with ADHD, who may struggle with selective attention (the ability to select and focus one's attention, while suppressing irrelevant or distracting information).

❖ **Apraxia:** a neurological disorder characterized by the difficulty in coordinating motor movements, such as speech, dressing, writing, eating, and other tasks. Individuals with this condition may struggle with controlling bodily movements. They may know what they want their bodies to do, but may be unable to plan or execute those movements on command consistently. Apraxia of speech is apraxia, specific to the area of spoken communication.

❖ **Aspergers:** is longer recognized as a diagnosis in the United States, having been merged into the autism spectrum, when 2013, with the publication of DSM-5, and other parts of the world in 2021 with the release of the International Classification of Diseases (ICD-11).

❖ **Autism:** Autism is a lifelong neurodevelopmental difference or neurodivergent brain type. It is present from birth, genetic, and may be masked or hidden by coping strategies. Autism is defined by social communication differences and a tendency towards what is often referred to by medical professionals as "restricted, repetitive behaviors" or, as I prefer, "a strong desire for order and routine in a chaotic world." Autistic people, generally, have noticeable differences in communication and body language (unless they are well-adapted maskers), which can lead to miscommunications with non-Autistic people. Autistic people often have Intense Interests in specific areas. As adults, they may be specialists or experts in their fields due to their dedication to a particular, often highly specialized, topic. These interests may be all the Autistic person thinks or talks about.

❖ **Demand avoidance:** Avoidance of everyday demands and expectations to an extreme extent, due to anxiety and strong need for autonomy. This extreme avoidance can even cause a person to avoid tasks they love or want to complete, if those tasks begin to feel like demands.

❖ **Distractibility:** Difficulty blocking out distractions in order to focus on work or tasks, with attention that may quickly shift from one topic or idea to another.

❖ **Dyscalculia:** A learning disability impacting a person's ability with math. Adults with Dyscalculia may take longer when working with numbers, may struggle telling time, or maybe more prone to making mistakes in calculations. While this can cause difficulties in these areas, people with Dyscalculia often have strengths in other areas, including (but not limited to) creativity, problem-solving, strategic and intuitive thinking, and a love of words and writing.

✤ **Dyslexia:** A learning disability that involves difficulty in learning to read and interpret words and letters. Dyslexic people process information differently from non-dyslexics, and many think mainly in pictures instead of words. Dyslexic people may be good at problem-solving and making connections. They may also be creative, imaginative, and curious, and many experience multidimensional perception (also known as three-dimensional thinking.

✤ **Dyspraxia:** Dyspraxic individuals often have difficulties in planning and completing fine and gross motor tasks, including tasks requiring balance and coordination. Dyspraxic people may also be empathetic, creative, out-of-the-box thinkers.

✤ **Executive functioning:** Much like the executive of a company helps to outline and oversee organizational functions and goals, executive functioning is an individual person's cognitive ability to manage oneself, by planning, and monitoring one's resources, in order to achieve a desired goal. Some NeuroDivergent people may struggle in this area.

✤ **Emotional overload:** NeuroDivergent people sometimes can have intense emotional experiences. Emotional overloads can come from having strong feelings that are difficult to manage, or when we have too many emotions happening at once.

✤ **Fidgeting:** All humans will experience fidgeting from time to time, but NeuroDivergent people often fidget more. Common examples include foot taping, strumming your fingers, hair chewing, and pen clicking, to name a few. Fidgeting is a way to release anxious energy, and can be a physical manifestation of concentration, anxiety, or stress.

✤ **Hyperlexia:** Hyperlexia is when a child can read at levels far beyond those expected for their age. Hyperlexic young people often will have a strong preference for letters and books, read early, without being taught, and may teach themselves to decode or sound out words at an early age, but may not comprehend what they're reading.

✤ **Hyperactivity:** People who experience hyperactivity may seem to move about constantly. They may exhibit extreme restlessness, pace, tap, fidget, or experience difficulty keeping quiet, overhauling, or speaking out of turn.

✤ **Hyperfocus:** is a phenomenon in which one becomes completely absorbed in a task. When one archives this level of deep focus, they are "in the zone", time can become distorted, and the rest of the world can seem far away. Hyperfocus typically occurs when a person becomes deeply engrossed in an activity that they are well suited for, or that they find fun or engaging.

✤ **Impulse control:** The degree to which a person can resist the urge to act upon a temptation, desire, or an impulse. Some types of NeuroDivergence can impact impulse control. Also, a person's impulse control ability can vary from day to day.

✢ **Meltdown:** A meltdown is a neurological medical emergency, like a seizure. It is an intense response to an overwhelming situation (such as sensory, emotional, or physical pain). A person having a meltdown may experience a temporary loss of control. Meltdowns are triggered by the amygdala flooding the brain with adrenaline. Meltdowns are the "fight" in "fight, flight, freeze, fawn". In both meltdowns and shutdowns, an NeuroDivergent Person's brain becomes so overwhelmed that they cannot access all of their typical cognitive functions. Someone in a meltdown may become angry, yell, throw, punch (themselves, others, objects), cry, or say things they would not ever say in normal circumstances. To help, create a safe environment where the person can ride the meltdown out. Be kind and realize the person having the meltdown is in a temporary state of panic.

✢ **Neurodiversity:** Coined and conceptualized by Judy Singer: The theory that diverse neurological conditions and learning disabilities are the result of normal variations in human brains. NeuroDiversity is important because it gives us a new way of viewing people with brain differences, in a non-pathological way. Neurodiversity rejects the idea that Autism and other neurological processing differences should be cured, and challenges the prevailing views that neurological diversity is inherently pathological.

✢ **Neurodivergent:** Coined by Kassiane Asasumasu: Someone who's brains diverge from what is considered "typical" for the time and culture they are living in.

✤ **Neurodiverse:** A group of people with diverse brains is a Neurodiverse group of people. A single person cannot be Neurodiverse. Neurodiverse groups of people include both NeuroDivergents and neurotypicals.

✤ **Neuromajority:** Coined by Dr. Nick Walker: Those who are not considered to be part of the neurominority.

✤ **Neurominority:** Coined by Dr. Nick Walker: A group who share the same divergence (e.g., Autistic, ADHD, OCD, dyslexic; etc.), where the neurotypical majority tends to respond with prejudice, discrimination, or oppression.

✤ **Neurotypical:** Those are considered to have an "average" or "typical" brain, for the time and culture they are living in.

✤ **Neurotype:** your brain type. **For example:** Autistic, ADHDer, Dyslexic, Dyspraxic, Hyperlexic, Neurotypical, etc.

✤ **Obsessive Compulsive Disorder (OCD):** Those with this Neurotype (which is a common co-occurrence in NeuroDivergent people) may experience hypervigilance, overthinking/repeatedly going over thoughts, compulsive ritualistic (anxiety driven) behavior. People who have OCD can be attentive and may have great attention to detail.

✤ **Palilalia:** whereas echolalia is the repetition of other people's words (or other sounds in the environment), palilalia is the repetition of the speaker's own words or phrases, for a varied number of repeats that may trail off at the end.

❖ **Reasonable accommodations:** adjustments to a workplace environment, policy, or procedure, that enable people with disabilities to perform their job tasks efficiently and productively.

❖ **Rejection sensitivity:** (common in ADHD and others who have been rejected by their peers repeatedly over their lifetimes) is the tendency to anxiously expect, readily perceive, and strongly react to social rejection. People who experience rejection sensitivity experience severe emotional sensitivity and pain when rejection (or perceived rejection) occurs.

❖ **Sensory overload:** Sensory overload happens when you're getting more input from your seven senses than your brain can process at that particular time. People's sensory quota can vary from day to day.

❖ **Sensory processing differences / sensory processing disorder:** people with sensory processing differences experience over or under stimulation through the seven senses. Overstimulation can cause physical pain, sickness, and exhaustion while under stimulation can cause frustration and restlessness.

❖ **Sensory aversion:** Most sensory avoiders are oversensitive (hypersensitivity). They experience sensory input more intensely than those without sensory processing differences, and (reasonably) avoid the sensory triggers that are painful or overwhelming to them.

❖ **Sensory seeking:** Most sensory seekers are under sensitive to various sensory input (hyposensitivity). When we require more sensory stimulation, we may seek it through engaging with one's senses (taste, touch, smell, movement, etc.).

✤ **Shutdowns:** related to meltdowns (both are triggered by the amygdala flooding the brain with adrenaline). With shutdowns the "freeze" of the "Fight, flight, freeze, fawn" is activated. In both meltdowns and shutdowns, an NeuroDivergent Person's brain becomes so overwhelmed that they cannot access all of their typical cognitive functions. Someone in shutdown may go silent and unresponsive, cry, or curl up in a ball. To help, create a safe environment where the person can ride the shutdown out.

✤ **Stimming:** Stimming is characterized as "repetitive movements" that someone may use to help themselves cope with rising energy levels in the body due to an increased emotional or sensory response. With verbal or vocal stimming, a person might make noises, grunt, or repeat words, phrases, or movie lines, they may also hum or sing familiar songs.

✤ **Touretts & Tics:** people with Tourette's and other ticing conditions may experience compulsive, repetitive sounds or movements that can be difficult to control. There are many types of tics. Motor tics affect body movement and phonic or vocal tics are sounds or words created by someone who experiences tics. Anxiety, tiredness, excitement or stress may increase the likelihood of tic occurrence.

✤ **Time blindness:** (common in both Autistics & ADHDers), those who experience time blindness may struggle to know how much time has passed and how quickly time is passing.

✢ **Working memory:** the ability to hold short-term information or other directions in your head, and then recall the information later, so that one can perform tasks or assignments. Everyone's capacity for working memory is different, and some NeuroDivergent people have extremely limited working memory capacity.

Workplace NeuroDiversity Rising [1]© 2022 by Lyric Lark Rivera [2]is licensed under CC BY-NC-SA 4.0[3]

---

1. http://books2read.com/NeuroDiversity-Rising

2. http://neurodivergentconsulting.org/

3. http://creativecommons.org/licenses/by-nc-sa/4.0/?ref=chooser-v1

Don't miss out!

Visit the website below and you can sign up to receive emails whenever Lyric Rivera publishes a new book. There's no charge and no obligation.

https://books2read.com/r/B-A-DKKV-RPDCC

BOOKS 2 READ

Connecting independent readers to independent writers.

About the Author

Lyric Rivera (they/them) is an autistic self-advocate from Texas, who runs the NeuroDiversity lifestyle blog "NeuroDivergent Rebel". They are also the founder of NeuroDivergent Consulting.

Lyric is known as the pioneer of the #AskingAutistics hashtag, where simple questions prompt open-ended responses that autistic people can easily chime in with, and invites participants to engage each other in conversations related to the topic. This hashtag connects NeuroDivergent people who would not otherwise have a reson to engage with each other, and fosters collective understanding of the autistic experience.

Read more at https://neurodivergentrebel.com.

Lightning Source UK Ltd.
Milton Keynes UK
UKHW011958021222
413123UK00001B/105

9 798215 235652